C. S. Lewis, MY GODFATHER

Letters, Photos and Recollections

Laurence Harwood

IVP Books

An imprint of InterVarsity Press
Downers Grove, Illinois

InterVarsityPress
P.O. Box 1400, Downers Grove, IL 60515-1426
World Wide Web: www.ivpress.com
E-mail: email@ivpress.com

InterVarsity Press® is the book-publishing division of InterVarsity Christian Fellowship/USA®, a student movement active on campus at hundreds of universities, colleges and schools of nursing in the United States of America, and a member movement of the International Fellowship of Evangelical Students. For information about local and regional activities, write Public Relations Dept., InterVarsity Christian Fellowship/USA, 6400 Schroeder Rd., P.O. Box 7895, Madison, WI 53707-7895, or visit the IVCF website at <www.intervarsity.org>.

Design:Cindy Kiple
Cover images: three photos: courtesy of Laurence Harwood
   frame: Nicholas Belton/iStockphoto
   pen and paper: iStockphoto

ISBN 978-0-8308-3498-3

Printed in the United States of America ∞

Library of Congress Cataloging-in-Publication Data

Harwood, Laurence, 1933-
 C.S. Lewis, my godfather : letters, photos, and recollections /
Laurence Harwood.
  p. cm.
 Includes bibliographical references.
 ISBN-13: 978-0-8308-3498-3 (alk. paper)
 1. Lewis, C. S. (Clive Staples), 1898-1963. 2. Authors,
English—20th century—Biography. 3. Lewis, C. S. (Clive Staples),
1898-1963—Correspondence. 4. Authors, English—20th
century—Correspondence. 5. Harwood, Laurence, 1933—Family. I.
Lewis, C. S. (Clive Staples), 1898-1963. II. Title.
 PR6023.E926Z674 2007
 823'.912—dc22   *2007031444*

P	20	19	18	17	16	15	14	13	12	11	10	9	8	7	6	5	4	3	2	1
Y	21	20	19	18	17	16	15	14	13	12	11	10	09	08	07					

Contents

1

INTRODUCTION

It has often been suggested to me, following talks I have given in England and the United States about my memories of C. S. Lewis as a godfather, that I should write down my recollections so as to provide a more permanent record of them for posterity. What follows is my attempt to do this and is also a personal testament to the man, based largely on memories stirred by a number of personal letters written to me, my parents and others throughout his lifetime. Focusing on their correspondence, this book takes time to describe my godfather's friendship with my father and mother, for it was as a consequence of this that I had the great good fortune of becoming his godson.

It is in the nature of things that most godparents are soon gone and forgotten once their charges reach adulthood. In my own case this was certainly not so, for Lewis was to be a significant influence on my life until his death in 1963. As a constant friend of my father, moreover, he was a regular visitor to our various homes during my childhood, visits which we all looked forward to and enjoyed. With my siblings and me, he used to join in our childish activities with gusto and took our play seriously; he talked with us, not down to us. When the family played at inventing telegrams or limericks, he always came up with the wittiest and most masterly contributions. His thank-you letters to my mother after such visits were often written in sonnet form. Further, his letters to me over the years were always pitched at just about the right level for my understanding; it was exciting to receive them, and I cherished them carefully.

With the passage of time, fewer and fewer people remain alive who knew him as a living friend. Therefore it is right and timely to record some of my memories of my relationship with the man and some aspects of his much longer friendship with my own father and with his contemporaries throughout his life, and with my mother too. It was through this friendship with my parents that Lewis became my godfather.

My father was born in Derbyshire in 1898, the son of a Nonconformist minister; he was educated at Highgate School, London, and there he first met Owen Barfield in 1910, their friendship lasted a lifetime. In 1916 both young men won classical scholarships to Oxford, Barfield to Wadham College and my father to Christ Church College. But on leaving school, Cecil Harwood first saw active service in France as a second lieutenant in the Royal Warwickshires. He very rarely mentioned to us, his children, his experiences during the war; my oldest brother's main recollection was the excitement of finding, in our attic at Streatham, a pistol, tin helmet and knee-high boots; booted and tin-hatted with pistol at the ready, he used to march down the road to confront his "enemies" from the local school and announce, "Any more trouble and you will get shot!"

Struck with appendicitis, Father was dismissed honorably from his regiment. Thereupon he went up to Oxford in the Hilary Term of 1919, and that same year he met Lewis through his friend Barfield. Thus began the lifelong friendship between my father and C. S. Lewis.

FRIENDS AT OXFORD

My father, Lewis and Barfield soon became fast friends. Lewis gives a telling impression of my father in chapter thirteen of *Surprised by Joy:*

> Closely linked with Barfield of Wadham was his friend (and soon mine) A. C. Harwood of the House, later a pillar of Michael Hall, the Steiner-rite school at Kidbrooke (Sussex) and an anthroposophist. He was different from either of us; a wholly imperturbable man. Though poor, like most of us, and wholly without prospects, he wore the expression of a 19th-century gentleman with something in the funds. On a walking tour when the last light of a wet evening had just revealed some ghastly error in map reading (probably his own) and the best hope was five miles to Mudham if we could find it and we might get beds there, he still wore that expression. In the heat of argument he wore it still. You would think that he, if anyone, would have been told to take that look off his face.

But I don't believe he ever was. It was no mask and came from no stupidity. He has been tried since by all the usual sorrows and anxieties. He is the sole Horatio known to me in this age of Hamlets: no "stop for Fortune's finger."

Much later entries in the diary of Lewis's brother Warren (known as Warnie) provide a glimpse of his reaction on first meeting my father and record interesting conversations between them. In about 1930 Warnie describes their meeting at the Kilns, Lewis's home at Headington, Oxford:

I went in to College to bring out Jack and his friend Harwood. . . . Harwood proved to be a pleasant, spectacled, young looking man, with a sense of humour of a whimsical kind, to whom I took at sight: he likened our meeting to that of Livingstone and Stanley in the jungle: he is an anthroposophist by conviction and a schoolmaster by trade, but with none of the caste marks of his calling. I wish I had seen more of him, and hope to do so on some future occasion: but the worst of these Kilns weekends is that it is impossible to have ones talk out with anyone, and already I find myself sighing after the peace and quiet of Hillsboro. I brought Harwood out and J. drove the car. Before the others arrived I showed him the pond which needless to say he approved of: in fact we found ourselves seeing everything with much the same eye. When J. arrived we did the tour of the estate, including the projected route of the wood path, and then put in an hour's reading at which Harwood did us good service.

LOVERS OF LITERATURE

A shared love of classics, myths and legends, philosophy and ancient history, Greek and Latin, English literature, opera and walking tours cemented the camaraderie of the three undergraduate friends during their time at Oxford—and for the rest of their lives. Together with other friends, including members of the Inklings group, they freely criticized each other's writing in poetry or prose; indeed Lewis continued to comment on his friends' literary work long after their Oxford days together. Lewis recalled how my father, Cecil, "danced with joy" on hearing parts of his own poem "Dymer" read out loud. A poem by my father, "Day and Night," received a frank review in a letter of July 1936 from Lewis; at the time my father was living in Streatham and had clearly borrowed (and not yet returned) Charles Williams's novel titled *The Place of the Lion*. The relevant stanzas in Cecil's poem are these:

> When I straighten my body into my bed at night,
> And the smooth sheet flows like white surf to my chin,
> I creep back into the womb of the world mother:

I shut consciously the lids of my eyes,
I spiritually close the gates of the sense of hearing,
I forget all touch and taste and the intake of breath and I wait.

And suddenly I swim through the waters of the flood;
There is no rainbow, and I stand in another light in Eden;
The souls of the animals fawn about me
Nor am I afraid of their vast shapes and great variety.
I eat of the plant before it has become root or stem or flower,
I play with light like fine sand and let it drift through my fingers,
I do not hear but I am music
And I know that if it ceased I would not be. . . .

"Jack" Lewis, as he was known to all his friends, wrote as follows:

How nice to get poems again! It was a bit of a shock to find you writing vers libre just as if you were beardless and modern, but that poem is the best of the three all the same: specially in the second stanza ("there is no rainbow" "light like fine sand" are lovely). The first stanza doesn't work with me because I never have resisting lids nor close them consciously and my eyes at bedtime are hungry for darkness not light.

Then he provided a bit of verse of his own in limerick form:

*There was a young person of Streatham
Who said to his friends when he met 'em
"Old Lewis is dyin'
For the* Place of the Lion
But I keep people's books once I get 'em.

Have a heart!

Yours
C. S. Lewis.

Ubi est leonis locus
*Caecilii lar et focus**

Correspondence of this kind between the friends maintained their friendship after they went down from Oxford, and there were frequent meetings between them to keep their special relationship alive. A letter to my father from Lewis's home at Hillsboro, Headington, postmarked March 1924, is a good example of this:

My dear Harwood,

I can see myself economising by a ride to London! One sets off proud in the consciousness of prudent poverty: and after five miles comes a glass of beer. Then comes the little roadside town with its white hotel and we have been so frugal up to now that at least we owe ourselves a good lunch—etc. I hope for better days; in the meantime you must come to us. The whole family moves to Clevedon on 3rd or 4th April. This sounds at first inconsistent with my refusal to come to London: but we have been lent a flat and all our healths need a change and this was partly in my mind when I refused you. If you can come down either before the 4th or after our return we shall be delighted—so see what you can do. Barfield and his wife were in Oxford yesterday and I had lunch and tea with them. He told me of your poem about Hodge—bring it with you when you come—it sounds a tit bit.

*"Where is the place of the lion?
The home and hearth of Cecil."

Πάντων μὲν αἰολούρων ἥδιστος πόλυ
Ὅδγης ἐμῇ γε καρδίᾳ πέφυκε πως !*

He had nothing of his own to show me, but we had a hilarious meeting.

An old fellow collegian of mine—Pasley—was here not long since and was expecting to meet you and Beckett. He is thinking of going in for an All Souls fellowship and—will you believe it—I have actually begun to think seriously of the same project myself. I don't mean, of course, that Pasley's design was the cause either formal or efficient of mine. I wonder would you mind getting some information from Beckett for me about it? I know that he is sworn under horrible penalties to keep some of the more ghastly secrets of the hidden circle into which he is initiated, but as I don't know the form . . . I ask at random. I suppose he is not allowed to tell what the thing is worth: but if he is, I should like to know—at any rate roughly. What papers are set? When are the exams held?—and any pertinent things he can tell me. He told me all this once before, I think, but I was not then very keen about it. By the way, am I technically eligible? I matriculated in 1917 and came back from war service in 1919.

I have a good deal to tell you but I hope to do so face to face—specially as a silly woman called in the middle of this letter and you know how that unsettles ones grip on the pen. Everyone sends their loves. We are perfectly well. ("Mr. Levett still keeps his place at my table"!) I have rewritten Dymer III and VI. I hope that the Secretary's Daughter of India will soon be able to give us some provinces to spoil, east of Suez. . . .

Yrs, C.S.L.

---

14   *Of all cats by far the nicest is Hodge, to my heart at any rate.*

Hodge was Dr. Johnson's cat, and what my father wrote on the subject follows:

Why yes, but through a Hodge, Sir,
    The present fancy feed,
I must to other mousers
    Affection's palm concede,
To kinder cats and wiser
    And cats of purer breed —
But Hodge is a very fine cat, Sir,
    A very fine cat indeed.

And while the glorious members
    Of the great feline seed
For tail or coat or whisker
    Win each a several meed,
For Hodge's general virtues
    A general voice shall plead,
For Hodge is a very fine cat, Sir,
    A very fine cat indeed.

What though the social column
    Be broken like a reed?
Though nought survive the ruin
    But Whiggish lust and greed?
'Mid total labefaction
    Shall stand the vital creed
That Hodge is a very fine cat, Sir,
    A very fine cat indeed!

Sir Eric Beckett, here referred to by Jack, was a close friend of my father and of Owen Barfield and often joined their walking tours; he studied law at Wadham College, was a Fellow of All Souls College from 1921 to 1928 and became legal adviser to the Foreign Office in 1955; he died in 1966. The "Secretary's Daughter of India" Jack wryly mentions was my mother-to-be, the Hon. Daphne Olivier, whose father, Lord Sydney Olivier, had been governor of Jamaica and became secretary of state for India in the first Labour government in the 1920s.

WALKING TOURS

The Inklings group, formed in the autumn of 1933 (as it happens, the year that I was born), consisted of several friends of Lewis who would meet regularly at the Eagle and Child pub—alias the Bird and Baby—in St. Giles, Oxford, to discuss, compare and criticize their recent writings. Some years before this practice was established, a number of these friends had already been sharing their love of walking in the English countryside; my father and Owen Barfield had been walking for a year or two with various friends before Lewis was invited to join them sometime in the 1920s. Thereafter Jack Lewis was enthusiastic in proposing walking tours to his friends.

These expeditions were marked by a degree of jovial formality, as can be seen in a suitably illustrated letter to my father requiring him to take on the role of Lord of the Walks, written by Jack in March 1931.

My dear Harwood,

I am instructed to inform you that at a meeting of the walk committee held yesterday in the rooms of the Union Society Oxford, the following resolutions were passed:

1. That Mr. A. C. Harwood be created Lord of the Walks, with all feudalities appertaining thereto: i.e. _sac_ and _soc_, _corvee_, _jus primae noctis_ vel nomanice, _droit de seigneur_,[+] _jus impune guitandi_, the high justice, the middle and the low.

2. That a petition be presented to the said Lord of the Walks on behalf of us his vassals, requesting permission to commute the said feudalities for rent or money payment: the said vassals to be declared, in return, free and delivered from all such services as the said feudalities imply. It is estimated that the said rent would amount to a sum between £5 and £6; the denomination of the said sum, notwithstanding, to rest in the last resort with the said Lord.

That the following resolution or rescript of the Sub-Committee for ethical problems be forwarded to the said Lord: "That it is the moral duty of the Lord of the Walks to grant the petition of his vassals for the commutation of his feudalities."

3. That the Walk shall begin on the morning of Friday April 17th from Hay: and shall return to Hay through Builth, Rhayader, and New Radnor.

4. That the said Lord be humbly requested to notify his pleasure in this matter to the committee at his earliest convenience.

In nominee sanctae et individui triritatis.

Of <u>course</u> you'll come. Hoity toity. What has that Captain Field been about not to leave a period open.

Yrs. C. S. Lewis.

⁺N.B. The said Lord, however, shall have no right to command the marriage of any of his vassals during the Walk.

Vassales facientes homagium Domino de Ambulationibus

Lewis once wrote for the dust jacket of *Perelandra:* "My happiest hours are spent with three or four old friends in old clothes tramping together and putting up in small pubs—or else sitting up till the small hours talking . . ." Walking was also always a favorite pastime of my father, and he used often to tell us of the joy he took from the companionship of friends like Barfield and Lewis on these occasions. From time to time they would explore farther afield, and Lewis would sometimes reconnoiter prospective lodgings and new walking prospects and report his findings, as in a letter written in 1932 describing the discovery of a cottage called French Court at Pett, near Hastings:

My dear Harwood,

The cottage called French Court is at Pett, about four miles from Hastings. The terms are two guineas a week. The sanitation is outdoor but aqueous not terrene. The hausfrau, Miss Carne, is rather an old maid but feeds you excellently; she is very mean about firing,* but contrariwise you have permission to gather firewood for yourself in the

---

**That is, "provided insufficient fuel."*

woods behind the house and two rather pleasant forage journeys in the day giving a racy practical flavour to your woodland walk and mystically incorporating you from mere tripper-hood into the body of rural life— will keep the sitting room warm. The beds are soft, level and clean. Water, sparingly supplied: you can get as much as you like from the pond at the back, but not of course for drinking. Miss C. converts this pond into drinking water by the process of straining it thro' muslin— which, I take it, removes nothing save what is beneficial. In my morning's washing water I looked down and "oh happy living things I said and blessed them unawares." (By the way the drinking water may come from a separate well—I rely on our maid's statement about the muslin, and on conjecture for its pond origin.) The cottage is beautiful. The wood is heavenly. The beach about a mile and a half distant and stony, flat, straight, much divided by groynes, and backed by the sordid beginnings of enterprise. Bungalows are numerous. The country is slightly deflowered by man, just the little that spoils it—a kettle not in every stream but about in every third—orange peel not in the secretest haunts of the wood but in the more obvious glades. The neighbouring towns of Rye and Winchelsea are of course among the three or four best towns I've seen—specially Rye . . .

Certain rules for these walking tours were established, predominantly by Jack. He insisted that lunch should if at all possible always be taken in a public house as he detested sandwiches, and he would occasionally stride out ahead of the others in order to reach the hostelry in good time. On one such occasion a rather steep hill had to be negotiated before the pub could be reached; Lewis did not like heights, so while his companions manfully started the ascent, he took advantage of a convenient railway tunnel through the hill as a shortcut and got to the pub well ahead of his friends, having shared the tunnel with a passing steam train. When they arrived, they found him happily ensconced at the pub with his pint of beer—but black from head to foot with railway soot! Barfield recalled that these lunches were usually simple bread, cheese and beer; however, when the order was being given Lewis invariably piped up with "And could we, in about ten minutes, have a large pot of tea?"

That Jack Lewis relished these perambulations with Owen Barfield, my father and other friends is abundantly clear from the enthusiastic manner in which he reported them to his brother, Warnie, for example. The rhythm of walking stimulated these friends' conversation and sharpened their considerable intellectual and literary prowess in a special way which Lewis clearly delighted in. In a letter to his brother on April 26, 1927, he gives a lengthy description of one such outing along the Icknield Way on the Berkshire Downs with Barfield, my father and Captain Walter "Wof" Field, a friend and colleague of my father whom he had first met in a shell-damaged village during the war in northern France. They were both in the Warwickshire Battalion, and Captain Field was a tall, thin man wearing a pince-nez who had achieved something like fame through his brave action in taking a German machine-gun station single-handed, armed with nothing but his officer's cane—a story written up at the time by A. A. Milne, titled "The Stick." Lewis writes:

> I was joined at Oxford station by two others and we proceeded
> together to Goring. One of them was new to the game and turned
> up carrying a Tommies pack filled square like a tommy's pack,
> for inspection. On the way we extracted from it a large overcoat,

a sponge, four shirts, a heavy tin mug holding about a pint, two strong metal cigarette cases of pudaita proportions and a number of those insane engines which some people associate with holidays. You know—the adaptable clasp knife which secretes a fork at one end and a spoon at the other, but in such a way that you could never really use the fork and the spoon together. . . . Having recovered from our delighted laughter and explained that we were going to walk in an English country and not in Alaska, we made up the condemned articles into a parcel wh. we compelled him to post home from Goring. It weighed about seven pounds. Our fourth met us at Goring.

After tea in the garden of the lock keeper at Goring lock—we ate it sitting just beside the weir, dipping our hands into the water and enjoying the rush and noise—we set out N.N.W. In half an hour the sub-urbanity of Goring was out of sight. We soaked for a long

*time in a winding valley with all the bigness of downs opening up
behind and the richer Chiltern country towards Henley rising in the
distance. We were on the broad grass track of the Icknield Way, the
grass very short and fine and perfectly dry, as it is nearly all the year
round in these chalk hills. It was an afternoon of lovely sunshine
with a pleasant light wind, and a lark overhead displayed all its
accomplishments. That night we slept at East Ilsley which (I think)
you and I went through on our way to Salisbury.*

*We spent nearly the whole of Wednesday following the Icknield
Way along the northern edge of the downs, overlooking the Wantage
valley on our right. Around us, and to our left, the country had all
the same character: close smooth grass, very pale in colour, deliciously
springy to the foot: chalk showing through here and there and
making the few ploughed pieces almost cream colour: and, about three
to a mile, clumps of fir, whose darkness made them stand out very
strikingly from the low tones of the ground. The extent of prospect
was (or seemed to be) larger than any I have seen, even from the
highest hills I have been on—just wave after wave of down, and then
more of them, for ever. The air is very clear here and one sometimes
sees a hay stack or a farm on a ridge, so distant and at the same time
so remote that it is like something seen through the wrong end of a
telescope. We had tea at Lambourn and slept at Aldbourne.*

*Thursday opened with discussions. A survey of maps showed a
lamentable discrepancy between the route we wanted to follow and
the possible places for lunch. Then emerged the dark and hideous
prospect of "taking" lunch. Perfectly simple you know. Buy some
bread and cheese before we start and have lunch where we like.*

Makes you independent you know. Drinks? Oh, get a few oranges if you don't feel inclined to carry a bottle of beer in your pack for the first ten miles. I need hardly say that our novice—the Knight of the Adaptable Jack Knife—was entirely in favour of a scheme which promised to restore his original conception. I, of course, who had seen days spoiled this way before, was the head of the opposition. The wrong party won. We stuffed our packs with bread, butter, cheese and oranges. The only thing I look back on with satisfaction was that the butter, at any rate, was not in my pack. Then we set off.

The first mile made us thoroughly aware of the fact that the wind (wh. had been in our faces since Goring) had risen to a gale. The next three miles left no one in any doubt of the fact that when a strong wind blows in your face all day, it parches your throat and chaps your lips without cooling your body. We were now in sight of "Barbary Castle," a Roman Camp, for the sake of seeing which all this folly had started. The exponents of the "carry your lunch" school had now reached the stage of indulging in a quite unusual degree of praise of the scenery and the pleasures of walking tours, on "this is fine" lines. But long before we had reached the top of that disastrous camp they slunk in silence, and only the malcontents (Barfield and myself) felt inclined to talk. In fact we talked quite a lot.

When we reached the top we found ourselves in one of those places where you can neither speak for the hurricane nor open your eyes for the sun. Beyond the suggestion

(mine) of performing on the wind (and the Romans) a certain physiological operation disallowed by English law and by polite conversation, we were silent here. Turning up our collars and pulling our hats down hard on our heads, we couched under a scrannel gorse bush wherever prickles and sheep dung left a space, and produced our scanty and squalid meal. The appearance of the butter faintly cheered us (all of us except the man among whose socks and pyjamas it had travelled), but it was a sight that moved mirth, not appetite. The last straw was the oranges, wh. proved to be of the tough, acrid, unjuicy type, which is useless for thirst and revolting to taste.

The midday siesta (that great essential of a day's walking) was out of the question in that abominable camp, and we set off gloomily S.W., Barfield and I dropped behind and began composing in Popeian couplets a satire on people who arrange walking tours. Nothing could have been happier. At a stroke every source of irritation was magically changed into precious fragments of "copy." By the time we had walked three miles we were once more in a position to enjoy the glorious country all round us. Five o'clock found us descending a slope full of druidical stones, where we started three hares successively so close that we had nearly trodden on them, into the village of Avebury.

Avebury overwhelmed me and put me into that dreamlike state which is sometimes the reward of being tired. Imagine a green ancient earthwork with four openings to the four points of the compass, almost perfectly circular, the wall of a British city, large enough to contain broad fields and spinneys inside its circuit, and, in the middle of them, dwarfed by its context, a modern village. Obviously here was the capital of a great king before the Roman times. We had been passing British things all day—stones, mounds, camps etc. But it was extraordinary to find a Berkshire village inside one. Here we had tea gloriously, in the orchard of an inn: and took off our shoes, and ordered a fresh pot and more hot water, and fair copied the satire and lay on our backs and talked Oxford reminiscences and smoked pipes.

Then Wof—he's the jack knife man—did a sensible thing by returning after a moment's absence and saying "If you're not very keen on <u>walking</u> to Marlborough there's a man here with a milk cart who will take us in." So we sat among milk cans (which are just the right angle to lean against) and bumped and rattled along the Bath road (of Pickwickian and coaching memories) into Marlborough. Field is an old Marlburian but we were too tired to let him show us the sights. He told us however (what will interest you) that the fine old Georgian building which faces you as you enter the school precincts was an inn on the Bath road in the old days. Pleasant days they must have been . . .

The letter continues at some length in this wonderfully descriptive way and reveals how much Jack Lewis loved the countryside and how sharply he observed and remembered all he and his friends saw and did together on these long walks. This walk ended at Wells in Somerset, a distance of ninety to one hundred miles from the start at Goring, no mean feat.

Captain Field, much later on, must have felt some uncertainty about his suitability within this group of friends, but he received a charming letter of reassurance on that point from Jack Lewis dated May 10, 1943:

My dear Woff,

Thanks for your letter. You can dismiss all that stuff about "being out of the picture." The whole point about the Walk is that all the members are unlike and indispensable. Owen's dark, labyrinthine pertinacious arguments, my bow-wow dogmatism, Cecil's unmoved tranquillity, your needle like or grey-hound like keenness, are four instruments in a quartette.

Anyway, you are under a simple illusion. You notice when Owen and I are talking metaphysics which you (and Cecil) don't follow: you don't notice the times when you and Owen are talking economics which I can't follow. Owen is the only one who is <u>never</u> out of his depth. The thing is an image of what the world ought to be: wedded <u>unlikes</u>. Roll on the day when it can function again.

Yours,
C. S. Lewis

On April 29, 1930, Lewis penned a fine description of another walk with these friends in Somerset when he wrote to his great friend Arthur Greeves:

I wish you could have been with me on my walking tour. We motored from Oxford to Dunster, three of us leaving the car about five miles before it & the fourth driving on. It was about six when we did so and we therefore had a delightful evening "prologue" to the whole walk over moors with a ragged sunset ahead of us lighting up the pools: very like an illustration to Scott: then down into a steep valley, over a swift stream as broad as Connswater but only an inch or so deep above its rattling pebbles and so into the broad, empty, practically dark street of Dunster wh. stretches up to the castle.

Next morning there was a thick fog. Some of the others were inclined to swear at it, but I (and I soon converted Barfield) rejoiced to meet the moor at its grimmest. Imagine a wonderful morning following a narrow path along the side of a steep hill with gaunt fir trees looming up suddenly out of the greyness: and sometimes a thinning of the mist that revealed perhaps a corner of a field with drystone wall unexpectedly below us or a rushing brook, or a grazing horse. Then down into greener country and hedges for lunch at the village of Luccombe. In the afternoon the fog thickened but we continued in spite of it to ascend Dunkery Beacon as we had originally intended. There was of course not a particle of view to be seen, and we knew when we had reached the top only by the fact that we could find nothing higher and by the cairn of stones over which the wind was hurrying the fog like smoke from a chimney on a stormy day. The descent, largely guided by compass, was even more exciting: specially the suddenness with which a valley broke upon us—one moment nothing but moor and fog: then ghosts of trees all round us: then a roaring of invisible water beneath, and next moment the sight of the stream itself, the blackness of its pools and the whiteness of its rapids seeming to tear holes (as it were) in the neutral grey of the mist. We drank tea at the tiny hamlet of Stoke Pero where there is a little grey church without a tower which holds only about twenty people. Here, according to an excellent custom of our walks, one of the party read us a chapter of Scripture from the lectern while the rest of us sat heavily in the pews and spread our mackintoshes to let the linings steam off. Then after a leisurely walk through the woods we

*reached Wilmersham Farm where we found our car parked in the
farmyard and Field looking out of a window to assure us that there
were beds and suppers for all. We had a little parlour with a wood
stove to ourselves, an excellent hot meal, and the bedrooms—two in
a room—were beautifully clean. We had only made about 16 miles
but were tired enough as it had been very rough country.*

*Next morning when I woke I was delighted to find the sun streaming
through the window. Looking out I found a blue sky: the farmyard,
with hens scratching and a cat padding stealthily among them, was
bright with sunlight; beyond the long blue-grey horizons of the moor
rolled up to the sky in every direction. This day we made about ten
miles by paths across the open moor to a place where we met a road
& there Field met us in the car with lunch. A cold wind was blowing
by that time so we had our meal (as you and I have often done) in
the closed car with all windows up and had the sensation of snugness.
About two and a half hours after lunch, having done a very tricky
walk across heather by pure map reading (no paths) we were relieved
to strike the valley of a river called Badgworthy Water (pronounced
Badgerry). A glorious comb[e], deepening of course as it proceeds,
steep sided, with many rocks in it, and soon with dotted trees that
thicken later into woods; not of fir but of stunted oaks, so gnarled
that they give the impression of being in a subterranean forest of sea
weed, & the branches often coated with moss to the top. We had to
ford the Badgworthy; not v. easy as (like all mountain streams) it
will be 6 inches deep in one place and 5 feet deep the next: ice cold
and the bottom slippery.*

Barfield created great amusement by putting his socks in his boots and trying to throw them across a narrow place so that he shd. not have that encumbrance while wading: instead they lit in the middle and, after sailing a few yards like high-pooped galleons, lit on the top of a fall where they stuck, rocking with the current and threatening every second to go sailing down into a whirlpool beneath. I, who was already safe on the farther shore, ran down in my bare feet and hoiked them to land with a stick. We sat down for about an hour with our backs against a little cliff of rock, in the sun and out of the wind, to eat chocolate and dry and warm our numbed legs. The first bumble bee buzzed by us. The colours of the stream, broken by a series of falls above us, and floored with green, brown, golden and red stones, were indescribable. When we were dry we worked our way down the valley to Cloud Farm where billets had been secured by Field. Minto, Maureen and I had stayed here about five years before, so I had a great welcome from the farm people. This evening all four of us had a kind of formal philosophical discussion on The Good. I shared a room with Barfield. Lay awake a little while, listening to the noise of the stream which is only about twenty feet from the farm house: and under that noise a profound silence. The Exmoor farms are the loveliest habitations you can imagine.

Next day we walked down the valley of the Lynn and lunched at Lynmouth. The valley is very deep—about 800 ft.—and the woods on the side almost deserve to be called forest. The river—which again we had to wade—is much bigger than the Badgworthy and so agonisingly cold that at the first shock it is almost the same feeling as stepping into a bath much too hot for you. Lynmouth you know. After lunch our route lay along the cliffs through the Valley of the Rocks which I had not greatly admired: a place of enormous crags <u>without</u>

water is a little bit horrible: one needs a stream to give these carcases a soul, don't you think? Best of all was after tea when we struck inland again over the moor in one of those golden evening lights that pours a dreamlike _mildness_ over the world: light seemed to be a liquid you could drink, and the surrounding peace was, if anything, deepened by the noise and bustle of a fussy little narrow gauge railway, the only living thing, which had a train puffing slowly along it, all its windows turned gold in the light of the sunset. We saw several herons this day. That night we slept at Challacombe and composed ex-tempore poetry: telling the story of the Fall between us in the metre of Hiawatha. We had done well over twenty miles and felt immortal.

The next day was grey with occasional rain. We got badly lost on some rather forbidding hills & failed to meet Field for lunch: got a lift along a dull stretch of road in a lorry: had tea at South Moulton and motored to Exeter. Here, seeing the Cathedral all lit up and notices outside it about a performance of the Messiah, we had supper in great haste and rushed off only to find that the Messiah was next week and that the lights were on for an ordinary service. It was horrid to be in a city again. As Field said "After training ourselves for the last few days to notice _everything_ we have now to train ourselves to notice nothing." Next morning the party broke up, Barfield and Harwood motoring back North, while Field and I trained to Bournemouth . . .

The letter goes on to say that Lewis returned to Southbourne and intended to post this letter to Greeves as soon as possible. However, a further letter on July 1 that year to Arthur Greeves, written while Lewis was staying with Barfield at Long Crendon, recounts some rustic activities and the following news:

> *The Barfields have been making wine from the vine that grows on their cottage and next year when it is ready to drink we think of having a Bacchic festival. The adopted baby is to be the infant Bacchus. Harwood with his fat shiny face, on the donkey, will be Silenus. B. and I Corybantes. Mrs. B. a Maenad. B. and I will write poetry and she will compose a dance. You ought to come.*

There were occasions when Lewis was unable to join his friends on their walking tours. In April 1936 he was invited to join Owen Barfield and my father on such a tour but was unable to go, probably because he was busy correcting and marking school certificate papers for the Oxford and Cambridge Schools Examination Board. His apology for this came to my father as follows:

> *O Caecili care, jam*
> *Pridem tibi scripseram*
> *Me non posse non negare*
> *(Surgit aliquid amari!)*
> *Tuam invitationem.*
> *Diram examinationem.*
> *Faciendam habeo.*
> *Multos pueros aro!*

Which in translation means: "Dear Cecil, I should have written to you long ago that I just have to turn down your invitation. Something unpleasant has come up. I've got to deal with a deadly exam—and I'm plowing* a lot of lads!"

Without their friend, Harwood and Barfield spent the last night of their walk in the Red Lion Hotel at Basingstoke, Hampshire, and decided to submit Lewis to a little leg-pulling. In order for him to be readmitted to the College of Cretaceous Perambulators, he would have to sit for a reexamination based loosely on the school certificate. Their first draft of the exam included the question "Who were: Owen Glendower, Owen Nares, Robert Owen, Owen More, Owen Barfield, Vale Owen, Owain, Ywain, Rowena, Rovin', Sowin', Growin', Knowin' and Gloin?" They completed the examination on their way home, basing its questions on places and events shared with Lewis on earlier walks such as those described above.

Lewis was delighted with this and answered the questions as a schoolboy might, writing out the answers in the copperplate handwriting of his boyhood. There is not room for the whole set of questions and answers here, but the following excerpts give an idea of the exchange:

Examination Papers

Candidates must attempt at least four and not more than six questions

1. Write brief notes on SIX of the following:
   a. Goring Post Office.

---

*That is, failing some students.

b. The "warm comfort of Christian Religion."

c. Exeter Station.

d. Bread for the House of Lords.

e. Philocasius.

f. "He thinks I'm a Financier."

g. "If it isn't bacon and eggs, its eggs and bacon."

h. "I hold no brief for Humanitarianism."

i. The mystic word "caboodle."

2. Why are you the best map reader?

Lewis's Answers

1. h. These words were said by the Marques of Bath.

i. A caboodle is a name sometimes given to lavatories. We are told that there was a very beautiful one on Exmoor painted the colour of peacocks feathers. Some scholars say it was more the colour of the vault of heaven. Vault = Sky.

c. Exeter Station refers to the railway station at Exeter where the Cretaceous perambulators all went to come back by train. We do not hear much about it. Exeter = a town in the west of England

d. In this period the Lords usually had their bed baked by a ghost called Mrs. Hunter. If any Lord wanted some bread he used just to give Mrs. Hunter a glass of water because she did not know that she was dead. She was a worthy, upright woman and the Marquis of Bath and all the other lords had a great respect for her. House of Lords = Parliament

b. This what Zeno said when they told him about hell. Zeno was a learned Roman philosopher who did not believe in hell. Another famous saying of his is Never let yourself believe in anything untrue. He does not seem to have been a very healthy man as he was always fainting.

e. Philocasius was a Druid's arch. It was discovered in a pigs' stye. In connection with Philocasius one is always reminded of Fatuus Longus. Fatuus (lat) = fatuus, unpractical. (Note: Philocasius means 'lover of cheese' and refers to my father who was very fond of cheese. Capt. Field, WOF, being long and thin was referred to as Longus!)

2. In order to answer this question it is first of all necessary to know what we mean by a Cause. This was discovered by the world famous Aristotle. It is true that he was not such a good philosopher as Lord Bacon but ought we to laugh at him for that, no. We ought to remember that he lived a lot earlier when people were much less civilized. The philosophers who wrote in A's time most of them put down anything that came into their heads in a carefree way and Aristotles polished sentences and classical illusions [we] must have great improvement. Aristotles astonishing learning enabled him to discover that there were four Causes—formal, efficient, material and final

e.g.

i. The formal reason why I am the best map reader is because I have the best map reading faculty.

ii. The efficient is because I read it best.

iii. The material is my brains.

iv. The final is that we can find the way.

The questions and answers continue in this vein; most of the allusions are to events or discussions which had taken place on earlier walks.*

My father and Jack Lewis eventually got onto Christian-name terms with each other. In those days, this took a bit of doing; Lewis wrote on the subject as follows:

Dear Cecil,

There is one point in favour of pronouncing it your way, namely that trestle has really no other rhyme, whereas thistle already has <u>whistle</u>, <u>epistle</u> and <u>gristle</u>. Things are like that!

Not to be outdone, my father wrote in the margin of this letter the words *wrestle, pestle* and *nestle!*

Jack's letter ends with: "You left 2 cigars behind. You'll never smoke them now!"

On one occasion during the war in 1940 Lewis came down from Oxford to Minehead in Somerset, where we were then living, to enjoy a few days walk with my father in the Dunkerry Beacon area of Exmoor. In a letter to his brother, written in January that year, he gives a vivid description of this expedition, including his encounter with our large family:

I dined that evening with the Harwoods, and being "carried" back to my hotel by him at about 10.30 had the very unpleasant surprise of finding it locked up and silent as the grave. It was about ten minutes' work of banging and shouting and ringing before I was let

---

*In 1983 the Oxford C. S. Lewis Society published a limited edition of the entire paper, and Lewis's answers were edited with excellent explanatory notes by Walter Hooper

in—and during the time I had, as you may suppose, some "very uneasy sensations."

Next morning, leaving my greatcoat and suitcase at this hotel, and retaining rucksack and mack, I climbed the steep hill to Harwood's billet and collected him. His children are now so numerous that one ceases to notice them individually, any more than a scuffle of piglets in a field or a waddle of ducks. A few platoons of them accompanied us for about the first mile of the walk, but returned, like tugs, when we were out of harbour.

FRIENDSHIP
AFTER OXFORD

After taking his B.A. in 1921, my father returned to Oxford with Owen Barfield for postgraduate studies, and they soon settled in to "Bee Cottage" together, in Beckley, just outside the town. My father did not get such a good degree as his friend. Very soon after the death of Barfield, when I was preparing a tribute to his memory, I discovered a draft of a letter my father sent to him on the subject, which made for interesting and uncanny reading in the circumstances:

> *Hateful Owen,*
>
> *Hypocrite! Apostate! Dissembler! Liar! <u>Scholar</u>!*
>
> *Do you know what you have done? Do you know that you have wrecked my life and written failure on my future horizon? Cursed be the day when you were born and the night in which it was said there is a man-child conceived. Selah.*

The loathsome tidings amply thrust themselves upon me. I was standing quite happy and contented in the queue at the Princes Theatre, when Horatio strolled casually by. He greets me. I respond warmly. Then one remark and the first thunder is heard: "Congratulate Barfield for me." What on! "I see he has his First . . ."

The scene changes; we are in the tube and my brother, with magnificent gesture, hands me a Class List. The first name, by G-, is A. O. Barfield, Wadham. Then I am home: "There is a letter for you!" One glance at the handwriting is enough. God! I thought (I often think God!); does the whole world echo with reverberating Barfields? What's this? "Rejoicing but subdued"? I'll subdue him. I'll wither him with a glance—no a telegram. What shall I say? Sarcastic formulae rush upon me. "We are not amused." No! That has been said before. I have it—one word: "Scholar." That is all the telegram will say. I go to bed happy.

This morning the brain is clearer. No! he is not worth a telegram after all. The whole pack of Barfields together are not worth a shilling; will write to him, for I have a vision of my revenge.

It is fifty years hence. Another eminent figure has been lost to the literary world. My son (I will beget one for the purpose) on whom some part of the mantle of his father has descended, is writing an obituary, I think for the Morning Post. The last paragraph rushes before me: "But although there will always be a few who will read Owen Barfield's poems for their antiquarian interest and the vast knowledge of Greek and Norse mythology which they display, it is as a scholar that his name will live for posterity. We might apply to him (and as a Johnson scholar he would have been proud of the *application) the words used by the Great Doctor—"A robust genius, born to grapple with whole libraries." He may have been scarcely a genius, but he was certainly robust. His editions of . . . (but the vision faded for a moment) . . . would alone have sufficed for the life labours of two ordinary men. They display a patient and careful spirit of research unequalled in the history of English literature. But what are we to say when we have to add to these his magnum opus—the Monumental work on Colley Cibber?* His other works may grow obsolete—indeed there are not lacking indications that newer texts are already supplanting his editions at the Public Schools and Universities, but this will remain forever an imperishable heritage. Age cannot wither nor custom stale it. It is a mine of information in which future scholars will always be delving, and always be bringing some new gem to light. His friends will mourn a charming personality; the world will lament the supreme authority on the Great Cibber!"*

Thank you! I feel much better.

Yours ever,
A.C.H.

In his diary Lewis recounts his frequent forays by bicycle to see his good friends at Bee Cottage. Their great mutual interest was poetry, and Lewis valued my father's criticism highly. His own poems, which Lewis described as "original, quaint and catchy," were published posthumously in *The Voice of Cecil Harwood,* edited by Owen Barfield (London: Rudolph Steiner Press, 1979). After leaving Oxford my father took jobs in publishing in London; Barfield describes him at this time as "making a rather half-hearted attempt to turn himself into

---

*Colley Cibber (1671-1757) was born in London and was a well-known actor and dramatist. He acted in and wrote plays, which became fashionable at the time.

what used to be called *a young man about town,* and even the Bloomsbury set were not wholly outside his orbit." But a very different destiny was awaiting him.

Together with Barfield he had become a member of the English Folk Dance Society, and during the summer of 1922 both men took part in an amateur concert party touring some Cornish towns and villages. There my father met for the first time the woman he was to marry, the Honourable Daphne Olivier. She was one of the daughters of Lord Sydney Olivier, governor of Jamaica from 1907 to 1913. She had read the medieval and modern languages Tripos—the final honors examination for a B.A. degree—at Newnham College, Cambridge, and after taking her B.A. in 1913 had become a teacher. It was through Daphne Olivier that Cecil first heard of Anthroposophy (described later, on page 60), and he joined her for a course of lectures given by Rudolf Steiner in Torquay in 1924. Plans were being made to set up a school in Streatham, London, to educate boys and girls on the principles expounded by Steiner, and Daphne Olivier was expected to be one of its first teachers. Cecil Harwood was so impressed after meeting and hearing Steiner at Torquay that he at once became committed to Anthroposophy. In January 1925 the New School (later Michael Hall) in Streatham was founded, the first Steiner school in the country, with my father and mother as two of its original five teachers.

My father and mother were married on August 14, 1925, and thereupon they moved into a house at 51 Angles Road in Streatham. An epithalamium to mark the occasion of their marriage was written with careful calligraphy by their two close friends, Lewis's in Latin and Barfield's in English. Lewis's piece was translated for me by Barfield before his death in December 1997.

In Nuptias Daphnes et Caecilii, Epithalamion

Qualis in immensum iam iam mare vela daturos
Ille vale dicens dulces adfatur amicos
Pauper et ignavae nimium telluris amator;
Haeret: longe oculis sequitur de litore cymbam,
Dum licet, albenti zephyro super aequora vectam:
Tum solus villam repetit, solosque penates
Vespertinus adit. Ego Daphnen Caeciliumque
Haud aliter precibus foveo votisque remitto.
Vos manet—et maneat divom delubra fatigo—
Oceanus late ridens lunaque serena
Strata maris. Vento tumeant iam vela secundo.
Apparent μακαρεσ υησοι noctemque per albam
Dulce sonant unda crepitantia litora lenta
Refluit et viridi fulgore anfractibus aequor.
Iam per opaca potes ingens vidisse cacumen
Arborum nemorumque, comarum audire susurrum
Silvasque Hesperidum: ramos ubi pondere poma
Aurea declinant philomela ubi voce canona
Quae canit et cantabit in omne volubilis aevum,
Florem ubi non hiemes ubi gramina non terit aestus.
Hic licet, ut referunt, paucis quos musa perennis
Quos Venus et ridens ducit Saturnia iuno,
Queis intacta fides, quibus et sapientia rerum,
Hic licet ad terram proras devertere fessas
Per vada Sirenis resonantia: nec vetat ullus:
Virginibus quid non licitum doctisque poetis?
Hic fas egredier. Semel hic pede pressere fas est

Mortali immortale solum lucosque beatos
Visere, ephemeridae, divomque accedere fontes.
Forsitan et vobis gravis admratio mentis
Crescat dum reputatis: "Adhuc stat Pontus et aer
Stelliferique poli: solis lunaeque meatus
Haud cessant: mutatque vices iam frugifer annus.
Cur non Luna suum repetens pulchrum Endymiona
Ebria desiluit de caelo? Quove modo nunc
Non flammata ruit pereuntis Tellus amores
Caeli proripere et gravidas miscere ruinas?
Omnia more suo? Naturae foedera rerum
Immutata manent? Nec spectant gaudia nostra?"
O vires sanctos! Veneris sunt omnia motu.
Rorem perditum amat terra arida et amnis amator
Oceanum: Caelum oceanus: sic Forma volentem
Materiam; noctemque dies: sic corpus amicum
Incola mens, hominemque deus, lacrimasque voluptas:
Attamen in tanta fornace et turbine amoris.
Viribus ipsa suis pollens placidissima semper
Inviolata manet spirantis machina mundi.
      Ast non immemores veteris vos este sodalis,
Ast, dum vos teneat procul hinc gratiosimus error
Inter odoratus silvas ubi murmur aquai
Insula sancta sonat, multis ex fontibus unam
Ne temptate labris. Dulci ne credite Lethe.

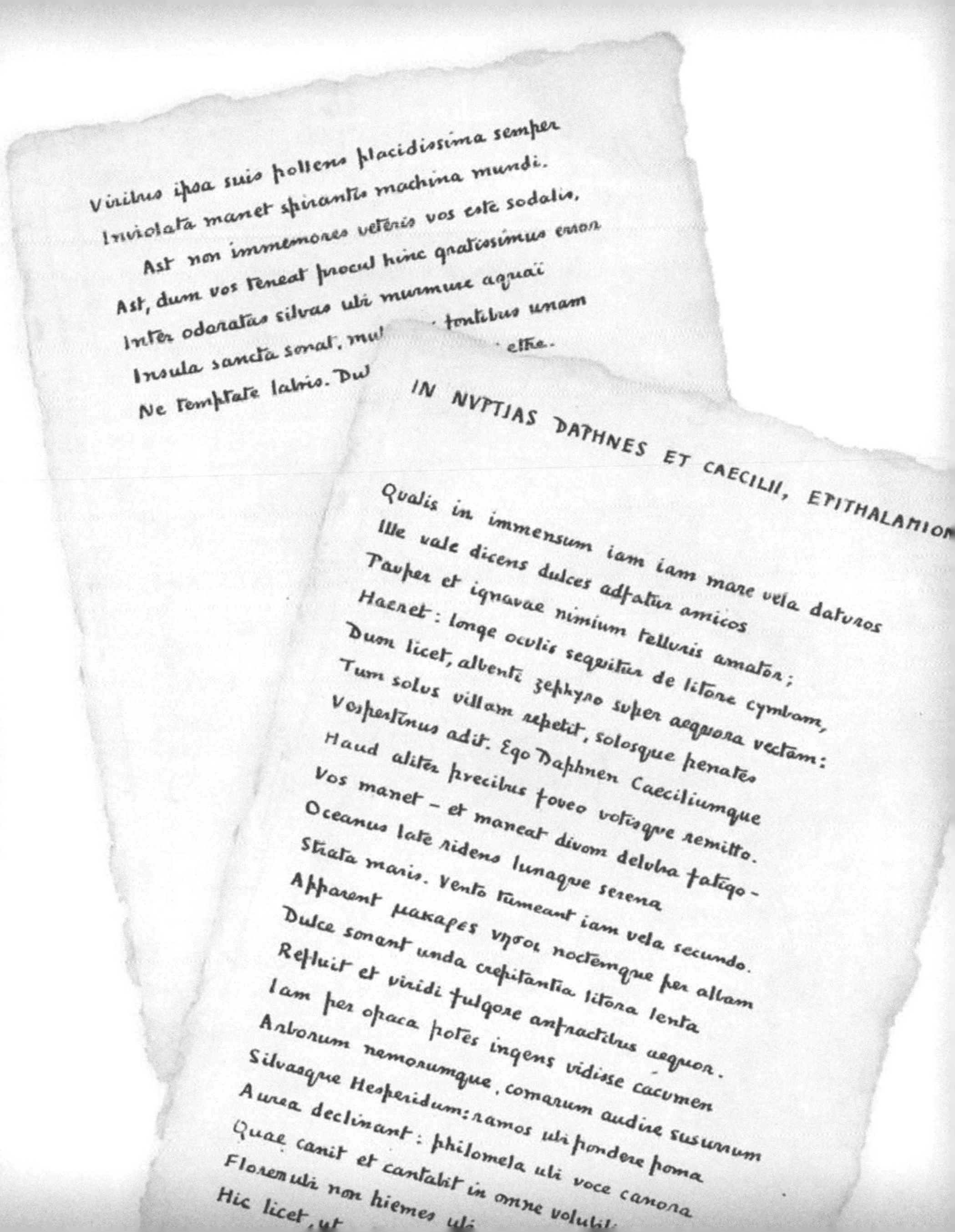

Viribus ipsa suis pollens placidissima semper
Inviolata manet spirantis machina mundi.
Ast non immemores veteris vos este sodalis,
Ast, dum vos teneat procul hinc gratissimus error
Inter odoratas silvas ubi murmure aquai
Insula sancta sonat, mu[illegible] fontibus unam
Ne temptate labris. Du[illegible] ethe.

IN NVPTIAS DAPHNES ET CAECILII, EPITHALAMION

Qualis in immensum iam iam mare vela daturos
Ille vale dicens dulces adfatur amicos
Pauper et ignavae nimium telluris amator;
Haeret: longe oculis sequitur de litore cymbam,
Dum licet, albenti zephyro super aequora vectam:
Tum solus villam repetit, solosque penates
Vespertinus adit. Ego Daphnen Caeciliumque
Haud aliter precibus foveo votisque remitto.
Vos manet – et maneat divom delubra fatigo –
Oceanus late ridens lunaque serena
Strata maris. Vento tumeant iam vela secundo.
Apparent μακαρες νησοι noctemque per albam
Dulce sonant unda crepitantia litora lenta
Refluit et viridi fulgore anfractibus aequor.
Iam per opaca potes ingens vidisse cacumen
Arborum nemorumque, comarum audire susurrum
Silvasque Hesperidum: ramos ubi pondere poma
Aurea declinant: philomela ubi voce canora
Quae canit et cantabit in omne volubil[illegible]
Florem ubi non hiemes ub[illegible]
Hic licet, ut [illegible]

A classical scholarly friend of mine (Mr. Ken Hodgkinson) has made some very interesting comments on this piece; what impressed him in particular was the sheer technical problem of organizing words into the quantitative hexameter meter for a start, then to handle Latin grammar, vocabulary and idiom, poetic phraseology, imagery and color within that quasi-mechanical and mathematical constraint, and, all the time, to give the poem, as a whole, a sense of progression and unity. He liked the neat tying up of the end with the beginning, the friend left behind, the engrossing pleasures, expressed with metaphor, imagery and mythological reference, leading to the final, rather wistful, mythologically expressed plea "Try them all—but not the waters of Lethe." (Of course they never did, or I should not be here to tell the tale!)

Any attempt at translation here raises problems—how much to just quote, how much explain? Cecil and Daphne are going to start a new life, so Lethe (the river in Hades where the souls drink to obliterate all memory of their former lives before being reincarnated) is more powerful than, say, the "waters of forgetfulness," meaning "Don't forget all the past, life, friends, shared experiences etc in your new life." A translation cannot get all this in.

Owen Barfield's translation which follows takes a middle path; he avoids transliteration, which can produce grotesque and fatuous-sounding English, and he does not attempt to create an English poem bearing little resemblance to the original. Instead he tries to reproduce the matter and substance of Lewis's poem, keeping as close as possible to the original while making the necessary changes of linguistic idiom to produce acceptable English prose, clothing it in well-chosen colorful vocabulary.

Epithalamium for the Nuptuals of Daphne and Cecil

*As when a ship is about to set sail upon the vasty deep, a poor timid
landlubber, saying farewell to dear friends, stands still and follows the
vessel as far into the distance as the eye can reach, where it is being
borne over the ocean by a whitening breeze: then in the evening
returns home to his villa and its familiar household gods. Thus I
cherish Daphne and Cecil with my prayers and speed them with my
vows. For you there awaits—I weary the shrines of the Gods (with
my prayer that it be so)—the sea's expansive smile and the paths of
ocean tranquil in the light of the moon. May your sails be billowing
even now with a lucky wind. The Isles of the Blest are in sight
and through the pale night their beaches rustle sweetly beneath the
impact of the slow withdrawing, greenly shining wave. Already you
may see through the mist a lofty summit of grass and trees, may hear
the whispering of the foliage[1] of the forests of the Hesperides: where
golden apples weigh down their branches, where the nightingale with
her melodious voice sings and will be singing. Ceaseless, for all time;
where winters do not destroy the flowers, or heat scorch the grass.*

*Here, as they tell, it is permitted to a few, who are guided by smiling
Venus and Saturnian Juno, whose faith is inviolate, and who are
wise in their dealings with the world. Here it is allowed them to
divert their wearied barque through shallows loud with the songs of
Sirens, and no-one forbids it. What is not lawful to virgins and
learned poets? Here it is right to disembark, here it is right for once
to pace with mortal feet immortal ground and to visit the groves of
the blest and approach the fountains of the everlasting gods, though
creatures of a day. Perchance in you too a solemn amazement may*

*arise, as you bethink you: The sea, the air, the star-studded vault
of heaven are still in place: the wayfarings of sun and moon go on,
and the fruitful year passes through season to season. Why does not
the Moon leap drunken from the sky, seeking her fair Endymion?
How comes it that the fiery Earth does not ravish the loves of the
dying Heavens and scatter them in pregnant ruins? What! The laws
of nature abide unchanged? Everything going on as usual? Do they
behold our joy?*

*O sacred powers! All motion is born of love (or Venus). Desperately
the parched earth loves the dew, the river, the ocean, the sky. So
Form loves willing Matter, and day loves night; so the indwelling
spirit loves the friendly body, God loves man, and pleasure loves
tears. And within such a furnace, such a maelstrom of love, the
mechanism of the breathing world, calmly relying on its proper forces,
remains inviolate.*

*Only be ye not unmindful of an old friend. As long as your
delightful wanderings keep you far from here, among fragrant
woodlands where your island echoes with the gentle sound of water,
out of many fountains leave one untested by your lips: eschew the
sweet waters of Lethe.*

[1]Comarum=literally "of the rain."

Owen Barfield himself entered into the spirit of this celebration of
my parents' marriage and wrote his own epithalamium for them in
English, beautifully inscribed with careful calligraphy:

Epithalamium.

Venus — or by some softer name
Let me invoke the gentler Dame
Thou art since thy last Babe was born in Bethlehem —
Seest thou these two young souls
Whom thy great planet rolls
Inwards together towards the centre of its sphere?
Oh now that tidal influence stem
And with more formal music escort them
(Not without help from my small pipe but chat)
To that grave gate more near
Which Hymen guardeth with his spear.

The _____ banner lately furled
_____ _____ _____ _____?
See them step stately — her who shall the _____ _____
Of him, who had the art
The soul's more conscious part
Into that western isle with England's laws _____ _____
With the soft feeling of the Nine:
_____ the latest of a stately line

Epithalamium

Venus—or by some softer name
　Let me invoke the gentler Dame
　Thou art since thy last Babe was born in Bethlehem—
　Seest thou these two young souls
　When thy great planet rolls
　Inwards together towards the centre of its sphere?
　Oh now that tidal influence stem
　And with more formal music escort them
　(Not without help from my small pipe but clear)
　To that grave gate more near
　Which Hymen guardeth with his spear.

The bloody banners lately furled
　This day across our gaping world
　See them step stately—her who shall the force combine
　Of him who had the art
　The soul's more conscious part
　Into that western isle with England's laws to bear
　With the soft feeling of the Nine;
　And him, the latest of a sturdy line,
　A stream which down the ages floweth clear—
　Self trusting, scorning fear—
　From Luther's pen and Cromwell's spear.

Oh, peaceful as our England looks
　When shine and shade outspread the stooks
　And underneath the sky old shepherds tell their tale,

Blest Goddess whom all praise
Give them these coming days:
A dream immaculate, a memory most dear!
What if unaided thou must fail?
What if thy strength alone cannot prevail
In this crass age?—yet have their friends no fear:
If lurking dragons leer,
Michael will guard them with his spear.

Behold them one by one take wings,
  The simple, safe, familiar things,
  Laughter, affection, even the vast truth Plato taught,
  While, wholly drowned in sense
  The body's excellence
  Two spirits learn in one wild shock too sweet to bear—
  First find each other whom they sought
  Then wake to find themselves anew, why caught
  In flesh, yet free—for mysteries light and clear
  Out of the depths appear
  Which Michael stirreth with his spear.

Thus, speaking out the word God spake,
  They steal new strength to give, to make:
  Methought I saw a chain of children hand in hand
  Which as in dance did move
  Through knowledge towards love
  And as they thridded, sang more shrill than chanticleer:
  A beautiful and joyous band:

Methought they thronged to save a palsied land,
Innocent, merry, wilful, wise, severe,
Self-knowing, cleaving fear,
And Michael led them with his spear.

And one, I dreamed, was doubly blest;
I knew him there among the rest,
Because through features strange, fresh printed on our clay
By heaven's conspiring hosts,
Peeped forth, like friendly ghosts,
Features not strange to me, not strange but very dear . . .
But whither, Goddess, whither? Lay
Upon these pulling doves some bridle, pray!
Descend—our task is present—joy is *here,*
Not in some future year:
Oh, let it make this pen a spear,

With which to tear the heart from verse
And lay it at his feet and hers
To step upon and float out into larger air:
For night draws on apace
And all must now give place,
The dusty frets with which this day their joy did smear:
Oh, sweetest Goddess, hear my prayer:
Now strew him roses on each soaring stair:
The door is open—see! the torch burns clear:
The bridegroom's self is here:
Io! Ho, Hymen, drop thy spear.

From time to time Barfield and Lewis would join forces to write verse, and to make it more challenging, even though often the subject matter was lighthearted, they would resort to Greek and Latin and send their efforts to my father for approval or criticism. A Latin and a Greek example follow, written from Long Crendon, Oxon, together with translations and comments kindly undertaken by Ken Hodgkinson:

Long Crendon.
Thame. OXON.

HAEC·FECIT·BARFIELD·OVENS·ET·CLIVVS·HAMILTON.

I. POEMA DE XVI ANIMALIBVS ARCAM NOE INTROANTIBVS.

Cum bove bos, sue sus, prae prus, cum tigride tigris,
Rhinoceros tum cum rhinocerote venit;
Necnon ridicula cum mure it ridiculus mus,
Tum Tom-felis cum fele, leone leo.

II. ΠΕΡΙ ΣΤΕΦΑΝΟΥ

Ἄξιος ἦν Στεφανοὶ βασιλεὺς μέγα κῦδος Ἀχαιῶν
ἠδ' ἰσοστεφάνους ἐπάκλς ἐπιείμενος ἀεί
καὶ δὴ φώνησας ἔπεα πτερόεντα προσηύδα
"Ὦ πόποι ἦ μέγα θαῦμα τόδ' ὀφθαλμοῖσιν ὁρῶμαι
Ὦνον μοι δεκτημορίῳ κῆρ λύγρον ἔθηκε ①
Λίην, ἠδε τομεὺς, κυναλώπηξ ἤματα πάντα ①

① Vat. μηδε ἴδοι τομέως τις κύντερον ἄλλο.

Haec Fecit Barfield Ovens et Clivus Hamilton

I. Poema de XVI Animalibus Arcam Noe Introantiens

Cum bove bos, sue sus, grue grus, cum tigride tigris
    Rhinoceros tum cum rhinocerote venit:
Neanon ridicula cum mure it ridiculus mus
    Tum tom-felis cum fele, leone leo.

Translation: I. Poem About Sixteen Animals Entering Noah's Ark

Bull with cow, boar with pig, crane with crane, tiger
with tigress,
    Rhinoceros with "rhinoceress" came:
Also silly little mouse with silly Mrs. Mouse,
    Tomcat with she-cat, lion with lioness.

This piece uses Latin elegiac couplets, hexameter and pentameter; the reference to *ridiculus mus* is a quote from Horace, "The mountains are in labor, and then out comes a silly little mouse"—a satirical comment on the spectacular effort of the writer for little result.

II. ΠΕΡΙ ΣΤΕΦΑΝΟΥ

Ἄξιος ἦν Στέφανος βασιλεὺς μέγα κῦδος Ἀχαιῶν
ἠδ' ἰσοστεφάνους σ/άκις ἐπιείμενος ἀεὶ
καὶ δὴ φωνήσας ἔπεα πτερόεντα προσηύδα
Ὦ πόποι ἦ μέγα θαῦμα τόδ ὀφθαλμοῖσιν ὁρῶμαι·
Ἄνον μοὶ δεκτημορίῳ κῆρ λύγρον ἔθηκε
Λίην, ἠδε τομεύς, κυναλώπηξ ἤματα πάντα ①

_____

① Vat. μηδε ἴδοι τομέως τις κύντερον ἄλλο.

Translation: II. About Stephen

Worthy was King Stephen, great glory of the Achaeans

and always clad in trousers Stephen-like.

And speaking he uttered winged words:

Oh dear, great wonder I see with my eyes.

The last two lines and the note in Greeck appear to refer to some in-joke.

My father paid tribute to his Oxford friendships in a poem he wrote in the early 1920s entitled "Nous N'irons Plus," which he dedicated to Owen:

Nous n'irons plus au bois,* no more, O friend O friend!
Our laurels are cut down, our glory sets behind;
And is it hard, when Heaven blows, for reeds to bend?
O we were oaks, and laughed at reeds and wind!

We shouted, and the Morning Stars together sang,
For we were sons of God and could there be an end?
Eden! And the Gate that murders with its clang!
And shuts us from the wood for evermore O friend.

In due course my parents had a family of five children; John (1926), Lois (1929), Laurence (1933), Mark (1934) and Sylvia (1937). After war broke out in 1939, Michael Hall School was evacuated from Streatham to Minehead in Somerset, where we remained until 1945. After the war ended, the school, which was also our home, moved to Kidbrooke Park, Forest Row, in Sussex, on the edge of Ashdown Forest.

Jack Lewis had been a regular and welcome visitor to our house in Streatham prior to the war and in Minehead during the war. After one such visit, he wrote to describe it to his brother, Warnie, on December 3, 1939, as follows:

> Harwood, owing to train difficulties, didn't turn up till about 10.30, but we sat up lateish and had a good talk.
>
> I may have mentioned to you that he has evacuated to Minehead—nicely placed for country but bad prospects financially, as the splitting up of their pupils' London homes has led to their losing a good many. His son John[*] is not with them but billeted in the neighbourhood—with the local M.F.H.![†] and already has acquired a new language and says that his father ought to get his hair cut! I hardly know which to pity more—a father like Harwood who watches his son being thus "translated" or a son in the process of such translation who has the embarrassment of a father like Harwood. I think the son: for as some author whom I've forgotten says the anxiety of children that their parents have about children "being a credit to them" is a mere milk and water affair beside the anxiety of children that their parents should not be an absolute disgrace. Certainly it would not be pleasant to have to explain to a M.F.H. that one's father was an Anthroposophist—except that the only impression left on the M.F.H.'s mind wd. probably be that your father was some kind of chemist . . .

When the school moved to Kidbrooke Park, Lewis continued to pay us regular visits. He always wrote the most charming bread-and-butter letters[‡] to my parents afterward, sometimes in sonnet form. In one thank-you note he expresses some jealousy that Owen Barfield and my father had walked together without him:

---

[*]*My older brother (not Lewis's son).*   [†]*Master of Foxhounds.*   [‡]*A thank-you letter from guest to host.*

I hope you will both come over and lunch. Barfield seems able to walk with you. You, happy man, are the common theme of walking whereon he and I are but alternative variations. "The one remains!!" My conversation with B. revealed the many slanders you have uttered against me. I am always being told that you say I say so-and-so, which I never said at all: and that you say you didn't say what I (truly) say that you said. This was a great scandal, in the etymological sense of a stumbling block or offendicle. I am a chewed string, a wrung floor cloth, an extenuated kipper, at present—cold, cough, wakeful nights, bad dreams, inferiority complex, bad reviews, unable to write . . .

Given that he was strongly drawn to the Norse myths, it is not surprising that Jack Lewis was a keen Wagnerian. He and his friends became avid opera buffs, and in 1934 Barfield commissioned my father on behalf of his friends to obtain seats at Covent Garden for Wagner's *Ring Cycle*. His failure to do so brought dire consequences from the pen of Lewis, who wrote as follows:

Dear Harwood,

It is vain to conceal from you the solicitude we feel for our seats at Co. Garden. Pray, pray, Sir, exert yourself. Reflect that no small part of the satisfaction of five persons depends upon your conduct: that the object of their desires is rational and innocent; and that their desires are fervent and of long standing. Omit no manly degree of importunity and complaisance that may achieve our object, and thus, my dear Sir, give me one more reason to subscribe myself.

[Y]our most obliged
most obedient servant
C. S. Lewis

For reasons unknown my father failed to secure the desired tickets, and when he wrote to report this failure to his friend Jack, he got this crushing response:

> Sir,
>
> I have read your pathetical letter with such sentiments as it naturally suggests and write to assure you that you need expect from me no ungenerous reproach. It would be cruel, if it were possible, and impossible, if it were attempted, to add to the mortification which you must now be supposed to suffer. Where I cannot console, it is far from my purpose to aggravate: for it is part of the complicated misery of your state that while I pity your sufferings, I cannot innocently wish them lighter. He would be no friend to your reason or your virtue who would wish you to pass over so great a miscarriage in heartless frivolity or brutal insensibility. As the loss is irretrievable, so your remorse will be lasting. As those whom you have betrayed are your friends, so your conduct admits of no exculpation. As you were once virtuous, so now you must be forever miserable. Far be it from me that ferocious virtue which would remind you that the trust was originally transferred from Barfield to you in the hope of better things, and that thus both our honours were engaged. I will not paint to you the consequences of your conduct which are doubtless daily and nightly before your eyes. Believe, my dear Sir, that I forgive you.
>
> As soon as you can, pray let me know through some respectable acquaintance what plans you

*have formed for the future. In what quarter of the globe do you intend
to sustain that irrevocable exile, hopeless penury, and perpetual disgrace
to which you have condemned yourself? Do not give in to the sin of
Despair: learn from this example the fatal consequences of error and
hope, in some humbler station and some distant land, that you may
yet become useful to your species.*

*Yours etc
C. S. Lewis*

Notwithstanding this merciless condemnation of his failure, it is clear
that my father at this stage sought an audience with Lewis in order
to apologize and make amends for his shortcomings. The next letter
reveals the masterly way in which Lewis dealt with his approach:

Sir,

*Your resolution of seeing me and receiving my forgiveness face to face
before you forever quit these shores does not displease me. As you
have rightly judged, to admit you to my house would now be an
offence against the grand Principle of Subordination, but you will be
welcome to the grounds—flumina ames silvasque <u>inglorios.</u>**

*You will please to observe the strictest propriety of behaviour while
you remain there, and be guided in everything by the directions of
Mr. Barfield.*

*Under his protection I doubt not that you will be able to achieve
the journey without any great disaster or indecency. Do not hold
any communication with your fellow travellers in the steam-train
without his approval: where you bait,*† *you had best abstain from*

---

*"May you humbly love the rivers and woods," adapting *Virgil* Georgics 2.486.
†*I.e., stop to obtain food or drink.*

*all use of fermented liquors. Many things lawful in themselves are
to be denied to one who dare not risk a further miscarriage. Above
all, do not attempt to save your guinea by travelling under the seat,
nor to shorten your journey by any approaches to familiarity with
your female fellow passengers. Do not bring with you any musical
instrument.*

Your obedient servant
C. S. Lewis

These exchanges give a good sense of the flavor of my father's
relationship with Lewis and his friends. Their correspondence
continued in like vein, as well as taking up much more serious themes,
throughout their lives.

Jack found it hard to come to terms with the fact that both Barfield
and my father and mother had become disciples of Rudolf Steiner and
confirmed Anthroposophists. Anthroposophy is a path of knowledge and
self-development that encompasses the realms of religion, philosophy,
art and science. Founded in what is universally human, it offers a
cohesive interpretation of human and world evolution, the reality of
spiritual worlds (of which this material world is
understood to be a part), practical methods of
developing an objective consciousness of these
realms, and deep insights into Christianity
and the world's religions and philosophies.
Steiner wanted no one to merely
accept what was presented with
blind faith; rather, he asked that
everyone test what was offered and

work in complete freedom with it. The philosophy that underlies the work of Rudolf Steiner (1861-1925) embraces a profound understanding of the human being and of evolution. People are rightly mistrustful of doctrine or dogmatic teachings that claim solutions for personal and world problems. There is no such claim in the work of Rudolf Steiner, which he called Anthroposophy. On the contrary, in presenting the results of his research, he sought to awaken individuals to their own spiritual experiences and investigations and to encourage a greater attentiveness to the manifestations of the spirit in everyday life. He described pathways of inner development that can be followed by each individual in full freedom. Anthroposophy finds practical applications in many spheres of life, including education, art, science, medicine, social science, history, philosophy, language and agriculture.

Lewis found his friends' position hard to take and often crossed swords with them on the subject. In chapter 13 of *Surprised by Joy* he wrote, "Barfield's conversion to Anthroposophy marked the beginning of what I can only describe as the Great War between him and me. . . . It was an almost incessant disputation, sometimes by letter, sometimes face to face, which lasted for years."

In July 1923 Lewis recorded in his diary the gist of a conversation on this subject that he had had with my father at Headington:

> Harwood and I lay under the trees and talked. He told me of his new philosopher, Rudolf Steiner, who has made the "burden roll off his back." Steiner seems to be a sort of panpsychist, with a vein

of posing superstition, and I was very much disappointed to hear that both Harwood and Barfield were impressed by him. The comfort they got from him (apart from the sugar plum of promised immortality, which is really the bait with which he has caught Harwood) seemed something I could get much better without him.

I argued that the "spiritual forces" which Steiner found everywhere were either shamelessly mythological <u>people</u> or else no-one-knows-what. Harwood said this was nonsense and that he understood perfectly what he meant by a spiritual force. I also protested that Pagan animism was an anthropomorphic failure of imagination and that we should prefer a knowledge of the real unhuman life which is in the trees etc. He accused me of a materialistic way of thinking when I said that the similarity of all languages probably depended on the similarity of all throats.

The best thing about Steiner seems to be the Goetheanum which he has built up in the Alps: Harwood described to me its use of the qualities of concrete which everyone else has treated in imitation of stone till Steiner has realised its plasticity and made it flow. . . .

Their differences, however, in no way diminished their firm friendship nor the great respect Lewis held for Barfield, of whom he once wrote: "Barfield towers above us all . . . the wisest and best of my unofficial teachers."

In a long letter to my father of October 28, 1926, Lewis explained more fully why he could not accept Anthroposophy:

Magdalen College, Oxford.

My dear Harwood,

*. . . About powers other than reason—I would be sorry if you
mistook my position. No one is more convinced than I that reason
is utterly inadequate to the richness and spirituality of real things:
indeed this is itself a deliverance of reason. Nor do I doubt the
presence, even in us, of faculties embryonic or atrophied, that lie
in an indefinite margin around the little finite bit of focus which is
intelligence—faculties anticipating or remembering the possession
of huge tracts of reality that slip through the meshes of the
intellect. And, to be sure, I believe that the symbols presented by
imagination at its height are the workings of that fringe and present
to us as much of the super-intelligible reality as we can while we
retain our present form of consciousness.*

*My scepticism begins when people offer me explicit accounts of
the super-intelligible and in so doing use all the categories of the
intellect. If the higher worlds have to be represented in terms of
number, subject-and attribute, time, space, causation etc (and thus
they nearly always are represented by occultists and illuminati), the
fact that knowledge of them had to come through the fringe remains
inexplicable. It is more natural to suppose in such cases that the
illuminati have done what all of us are tempted to do:—allowed
their intellect to fasten on those hints that come from the fringe,
and squeezing them, has made a hint (that was full of truth) into
a mere false hard statement. Seeking to know (in the only way we
can know) more, we know less. I, at any rate, am at present inclined
to believe that we must be content to feel the highest truths "in*

our bones": if we try to make them explicit, we really make them untruth.

At all events if more knowledge is to come, it must be the wordless & thoughtless knowledge of the mystic: not the celestial statistics of Swedenborg, the Lemurian history of Steiner, or the demonology of the Platonists. All this seems to me merely an attempt to know the super-intelligible <u>as if it were a new slice of the intelligible</u>: as though a man with a bad cold tried to get back smells with a microscope. Unless I greatly misunderstand you, you are (in a way) more rationalist than I, for you would reject as mere ideology my "truths felt in the bones." All this, by the bye, is meant for exposition, not argument. . . .

Following a visit to our Streatham home in 1931, Lewis wrote a bread-and-butter letter to my mother of the kind he was often to send to her after such visits; it is dated September 10, 1931:

Dear Mrs. Harwood,

It is recorded in the Laxdale Saga that Kjartan Olaffson stood up in the All-Thing and invited the whole of Iceland to his wedding—of which men said that it was "manfully offered." Your summoning of the whole clan to Streatham was a delightful revival of these old heroical hospitalities. I shall long remember the game of definitions and our later excursion into angelology: and for this, and the swings, to you, and to John, accept my best thanks.

I met your father in the train and learned from him that I should launch some minnows in my pond as an ally against the mosquitoes. I doubt if this will be as effective as the chemical measures which you suggest, but it is certainly less Ahrimanic. A league, even an armed league, with one kind of beast against another will be better fun than an invasion of all with the inorganic. My head is full of beasts at the moment because I am reading Jeremy Taylor from whom I learn:

(1) Not "to seek counsel of the prodigal and trifling grasshopper."

(2) That "it is better to sit up all night than to go to bed with a dragon."

I feel sure he is quite right. These old divines had a lot of sense.

Yours very sincerely,
C. S. Lewis

My mother inevitably got drawn into the debate over Anthroposophy with Lewis, and she must herself have written to him on the subject. One of his responses is contained in a reply of March 28, 1933:

> *Dear Mrs. Harwood,*
>
> *I hope it was not only literary vanity that made me enjoy so much your very kind and very discriminating letter. Thank you very much indeed. . . .*
>
> *I am glad you never read my* Summa,* *for all that is dead as mutton to me now: and the points chiefly at issue between the Anthroposophists and me then were* <u>precisely</u> *the points on which Anthroposophy is certainly right—i.e. the claim that it is possible for a man, here and now, in the phenomenal world, to have commerce with the world beyond—which is what I was denying. The present difference between us is quite other. The only thing that I now wd. object eagerly to in Anthroposophy is that I don't think it can say "I believe in one God the Father Almighty." My feeling is that even if there are a thousand orders of beneficent being above us, still, the universe is a cheat unless at the back of them all there is the one God of Christianity. But I did not mean to raise controversial points: there is certainly quite a lot for us to agree on as against nearly the whole of the contemporary world! I would quite agree, for instance, with your discovery that it is the* <u>Will</u> *wh. lets the cat out of the bag—and also with your refusal to rest in Croce. His is the kind of idealism that for all practical purposes is indistinguishable from materialism. What a ghastly pun that his name should mean "Blessed Cross"!*

Lewis's Summa *was a document into which he put many of his arguments against Anthroposophy arising from his "Great War" with Owen Barfield on the subject.*

I don't understand the part about the eternal feminine (and masculine) in your letter, and look forward to hearing more about it when next we meet. Cecil was looking grand when he came down to us—he is the most un-aging of my friends.

We are all disappointed that your father has abandoned the idea of buying Tewsfield. With very many thanks.

Yours sincerely
C. S. Lewis

Owen Barfield would occasionally impart his own views to my father on what Jack Lewis was doing. For example, in a letter dated January 27, 1941, he makes some interesting comments on Lewis's recently published *The Problem of Pain*:

My dear Cecil,

I shall be interested to hear your reaction to "The Problem of Pain." It has worried me rather, and there are elements in it which jar on me more than anything Lewis has written. It would not be Lewis's if it were not invigorating and fresh on an old subject written with beautiful sincerity. As to the jarring element, I should not myself call it dogmatic, rather magisterial and admonitory. I even feel a touch of pastiche in it—not deliberately assumed in the writing but a pastiche which he is living. I am wondering into what final shape his great intellectual and moral courage will harden his Weltanschauung. I feel it will take him wherever his notion of truth leads him—if

*necessary in the face of his own deepest prejudices. There is this
element of force in the way in which his own mind treats him, the
mind which treats other inferior minds with such surprising respect,
courtesy and tact. He might, in a previous incarnation, have been a
convinced inquisitor and now getting his own back on himself. But it
frightens me a bit. Whereas you or I would follow an intellectually
apprehended principle only to the point where it began to interfere
with our deepest prejudices, partly out of cowardice and a weak
willingness to temporise, but partly also out of a sort of pondering
wisdom, of which these prejudices are sometimes an expression (I
think Lewis is rather lacking in this, though he is quick to recognise
it in others), <u>he</u> would not hesitate to do violence to the prejudices at
whatever cost.*

*I find it rather difficult to express my meaning or, as Wordsworth put
it in those great lines in the Prelude:—*

*My drift, I fear
Is scarcely obvious*

*And this may well indicate that I mean less than I think I do. I do
<u>not</u> mean that I think L's Christianity is of the head and not of the
heart. On the contrary, the heart is just the truth he has frozen on
to. And I no longer fear he will finish up in Rome.*

In December 1963, very shortly after Lewis's death, Barfield sent
my father a copy of a "Biographia Theologica" he had written in
Greek many years before, during or before the war, concerning his
friend Jack, in the style of the opening of St. John's Gospel. It seems
apposite to include it at this point; Owen wrote that as far as he

could recall he decided not to send it to Jack, whose reaction would no doubt have been suitably trenchant and masterly and written in Greek in a similar vein!

C.S.L.

Βιογραφια Theologica

ἰδοὺ ἦν φιλόσοφός τις, καὶ ἔγνω ἑαυτὸν ὁ
φιλόσοφος ὅτι εἷς ἐστι. καὶ ὁ λόγος ἐν τῷ
φιλοσόφῳ γενόμενος ἦν εἷς θεός. καὶ ὁ λόγος
ἦν τὸ φῶς τῆς φιλοσοφίας αὐτοῦ· καὶ τὸ φῶς
ἐν τῇ φιλοσοφίᾳ φαίνει καὶ ὁ φιλόσοφος αὐτὸ
οὐκ ἔγνω. ἐν τῷ φιλοσόφῳ ἦν καὶ ἡ φιλοσοφία
δι' αὐτοῦ ἐγένετο. καὶ ὁ φιλόσοφος αὐτὸ οὐκ
ἔγνω. καὶ δὴ καὶ οὐκ ἔφη ὁ φιλόσοφος ὅτι
οὐδεὶς δύναται τὸ φῶς οὔποτε οὐδαμῶς θεᾶσθαι.
καὶ θεασάμενος τὸ φῶς ἐκάλησεν ὁ φιλόσοφος
ὅτι ὄνομα αὐτῷ κύριος. καὶ ἐμαρτύρησεν ἡ
φιλοσοφία περὶ τοῦ φωτὸς ὅτι λόγος καὶ ζωὴ
τῶν ἀνθρώπων ἐστι καὶ περὶ τοῦ φιλοσόφου
ὅτι οὐκ ἐξ αἱμάτων οὐδὲ ἐκ θελήματος σαρκὸς
οὐδὲ ἐκ θελήματος ἀνδρὸς οὐδὲ δι' ἐντολῆς
κυρίου ἀλλ' ἐκ θεοῦ καὶ τέκνου θεοῦ ἐγεννήθη.
καὶ ὁ φιλόσοφος τὴν μαρτυρίαν οὐ κατέλαβεν.

Found this today among some old papers. Wrote it
many years ago, during or before the war, & so far as
I recall decided not to send it to [...]

Translation: Behold there was a certain philosopher, and the philosopher knew himself, that he was one. And the word arising in the philosopher was one god. And the Word was the light of his philosophy. And the light shone in the philosophy, and the philosopher knew it not. It was in the philosopher and the philosopher was born of it and the philosopher did not know it. And indeed the philosopher denied that anyone could behold the light in any other way. And having beheld the light the philosopher said that its name was Lord. And philosophy bore witness about the light that it was the word and the life of men; and about the philosopher that he was not born of blood or of the will of the flesh, or the will of a man or through the order of a master, but from God and was the son of God. And the philosopher did not comprehend [accept?] the testimony.

In that month after Jack's death Owen Barfield also reminded my father of a poem by Jack which he had totally forgotten, and which was published in a slightly revised version the following year.

To a Friend

If knowledge like a midday heat,
Uncooled with cloud, unstirred with breath
Of undulant air, begins to beat
On souls one moment after death,

From your rich soil what lives will spring,
What flower-unfolding paradise,
Through what green walks what birds will sing,

What med'cinable gums, what spice!

Apples of what smooth gold! But
Fear is on me for myself. The noon
That nourishes Earth can only sear
And scald the unresponding Moon.

On her dry vales there is no soil,
Her needle pointed hills are bare.
Water, poured on those rocks, would boil
And noon lasts long, and long despair.

After my father's death in 1975 I found among his papers another (published) poem in Lewis's hand, written on Magdalen College, Oxford, notepaper.

Some believe the slumber
Of trees is in December
When timber's naked under stars
And squirrel keeps his chamber.

But I believe their fibres
Awake to life and labour
When turbulence comes roaring up
The land in loud October,

And charges, and enlarges
The breach, and lays his sieges,
And scourges trees till, like the bones
Of thought, their shape emerges.

Form is soul. In warmer,
Seductive days, disarming
The firmer will, the wood grew soft
And spread its dreams to murmur.

Into earnest winter,
Like souls awaked, it enters,
The hunter Frost and the cold light
Have quelled the green enchanter.

The topics taken up in the correspondence among these good friends ranged widely, as can be seen from the following letters written by Jack in the late 1930s and the 1940s with comments on writing in general, his fame, Christianity, Kipling, and my father's own work, including the following lines from a Christmas poem which Cecil had sent to his friend for comment, which was later published in *The Voice of A. C. Harwood:*

On a morn at Christmastide
Down a lane with plough beside
With a musing-quickened ear
I heard the turning of the year,
Like the dawn-sense or the knack
To know the tide is past the slack.
February brought in frost,

But that music was not lost,
March came in with deeper snow,
Still the sap would sing and flow,
And open senses caught the sound
In mid-March crocus ground.

Shepherds round the glowing coals
In their simple dreaming souls
Heard the song and saw the light
And knew what child was born that night,
Hearkening across the silent snow
His first warm cry of human woe.
The song ended, the light faded,
They woke hungry, they woke jaded,
Back the old life came again,
The misery of snow and rain
And longing for the morn—
But another world is born.
Earth is red with human blood,
Christ is come from Jordan flood,
Cities shattered, nations beggared,
He is on the Mount disfigured,
Men deny the human name,
He is risen as a flame
Leaps to spiritual form—
And another Man is born. . . .

Lewis makes the following observations
on this offering:

The Kilns

My dear Cecil,

Oh, very good. The poem I mean. I don't know that a certain winter and Christmas sensation of hard white shell and hot crimson kernel has ever been better expressed (at least until I wrote this very sentence!). I like the "dawn sense" and the "knack to know the tide is past the slack" very much—and the following paragraph about the shepherds. Unless there's some point I haven't seen "common senses" (wh. I take it means merely the senses of [Greek]) worries one by the suggestion of two inclement meanings; a) Commonsense b) "The Common Sense" of old psychology. By the way do you gain anything by the short lines at the end of para. 3? Thank Laurence for his picture: I recognised the subject at once. (This is a naif eulogy: but sound as far as it goes, specially in hac tenera aetate.) I shall be on tour, converting the R.A.F., all next week, so I'm afraid there's no chance of meeting. But at the end of next term (about March 13th) could we have another re-union at Magdalen? If we're still alive and (in some ways more important) still civilians. I have to spend so much time away from home on work now that I can hardly ever be absent on pleasure as well. But I also am "hungry to see and hear you again." If this won't do mention any date you like (in term time—it's impossible to have guests at the Kilns now) and <u>come</u>. I'll have a book to send you soon. My duty to Daphne—and oh! talking of lay sermons I've got to address The Senior Wives Association (did you conceive there could be such a thing?) next term. Not De Claris Mulieribus but ad claras mulieres.* It's like penetrating the mysteries of the Bona Dea.† Read John Galt if you want some good novels. Blessings on you,

Yours Jack Lewis

---

*Not On Famous Women *(a collection of biographies of women by Giovanni Boccaccio) but to famous women.* †The Good Goddess.

Elegy
(Written to prove that the Limerick metre is not irretrievably comic)

She was delicately, beautifully made;
So small, so unafraid,
Till the bomb came
(Bombs are the same
Delicately, beautifully made).

In another letter to my father written at about this time, Lewis comments on some of the problems of fame: "What I'm enjoying is Fame, Fame = spending all your spare time answering letters. It is *not,* as the moralists say, like dead sea fruit: it is much more like an imposition (in the schoolmaster's sense). As in a better world our very punishments will be rewards, so, in this vale of tears our v. rewards are punishments."

In 1940 Cecil Harwood published his book *The Way of a Child* on Steiner Waldorf education. As noted earlier, he was the first male Waldorf teacher in Britain, had been intensely involved in the establishment of Steiner education in its early years together with my mother, and had experienced the struggles and successes of his fellow pioneers. His time as a teacher gave him the insight to write this little book, which was based not only on his own experience but also on the study of Rudolf Steiner's books and lectures on childhood and education. He sent the book to his friend for comment, and Jack Lewis wrote to him from the Kilns on August 3, 1940, as follows:

My dear Harwood,

Many thanks for the Way of a Child. *It arrived while my brother was on leave and by the time I had finished it I had quoted to him so many of the plusses that he actually read it himself—a very extreme measure for him, considering the subject—and greatly enjoyed it. I liked it very much myself. In style (except for "makes a unique contribution" on p. 55!!!) it seems to me a model of exposition—so easy and even that there is nothing to distract one's attention from the content, and yet one discovers at the end that it has been full of life and humour. As for the content, I suppose the "highest tribute" (to prolong the style of your one lapse) I can pay is to say that it gave me a disquieting light on my own childhood—one of extreme intellectual precocity—and of its results in the present and so increased self-knowledge. Also, everything of what you say about children which came within my own observation seemed to be perfectly true. "You need two sets of tools" is specially happily put.*

I expect you have the same experience in writing that I do, now that we both have a body of doctrine we believe to be true. In the old days, when one was trying to be clever and invent an attitude, writing was the devil. Now it's more like doing dictation: you've just got to get it down and the course is straight. Rather like what you said about our canal walk "No silly mountains or scenery, all pure pleasure."

*Our evacuees have grown up and left school so we are now an empty
house. Maureen is going to be married to a man called Blake, very
ugly but a Christian and a good musician. Warnie is stationed at
Cardiff and has been twice up to us on leave and I have been down
to him for a weekend. I am an L.D.V.* (D.V.)† (This is as good a
pun as ever I made). Mrs. Moore is pretty well. I am reading a)
Juvenal, whom I somehow escaped at school. He has real tragic
power: e.g. of a tyrant's friends: Omnibus in facie magnae
miseraeque sedebat pallor amicitiae!‡ b) Lady Julian of Norwich
"Revelations of Divine Love." She was a corker. She seems to have
done for the reconciliation of Kant and Christianity what Aquinas
did for Aristotle and Christianity, with the trifling difference that she
did it some centuries before K. was born. How do you all go on? I
hope you have had as little direct experience of the war as we. Let me
have a line and give my love to Daphne.*

Yours, C. S. Lewis.

Having read *The Way of a Child* and shortly before writing this letter,
Lewis wrote to Owen Barfield, formally "exonerating" his three
Anthroposophical friends (Barfield, my mother and father), perhaps
with a view to ending his dispute with Anthroposophy and as a mark
of respect for his three friends. The letter is in rather formal terms:

*Though I reject (in so far as I understand them) the philosophy
and theology of Dr. Rudolph Steiner and the Anthroposophical
Movement, I have been intimately acquainted with some who adhere
to it for over seventeen years.*

One of them is the man of all my acquaintances whose character both

---

moral and intellectual I should put highest, or nearly so.

Another has written a book on education entitled The Way of a Child *which seems to me full of good sense.*

Another (perhaps the most enthusiastic Anthroposophical of the three) has continued throughout the time of our acquaintance to be an excellent mother of five children. The eldest son, who is not old enough for a judgement to be formed about the matter, appears to me to be an alert, healthy, civil and manly boy who reflects nothing but credit to his upbringing.

Believing the doctrines of Dr. Steiner to be erroneous (though not more so than those of many philosophers who are more widely influential than he in modern England) and being frequently engaged in controversy with my Anthroposophical friends on this subject, I believe I should have been very quick to notice any evidence that adherence to the system was producing either intellectual or moral deterioration. Of such evidence I have not found a shred. The friends of whom I speak are all highly educated people and I have not found anything to diminish my respect either for their characters or their capacities.

I should perhaps add that the works of Dr. Steiner are extremely difficult reading: unassisted popular opinion on them is likely to be no more reliable than the same opinion on Kant or Whitehead.

The correspondence continued spasmodically. Jack's letters were always of interest, raising points for debate or commenting on the writings and influence of other authors such as, in the following example, Rudyard Kipling.

---

78   *referring to the "Privy Councillors" summoned to a meeting with their tyrannical Emperor Domitian.*

Sometime about the 27th July 1944

My dear Cecil—

Your letter, which arrived when I did not feel equal to answering it has now suffered the fate of anything whatever wh. I venture to leave on my table for more than 24 hours, and disappeared. <u>Did</u> you say anything in it about the young lady who wants lodging—the one about whom you wrote to Mrs. Moore yesterday? I can't remember a word on <u>that</u> subject. At any rate that's alright. A Mrs. Dodwell (Marcia is her Christian name, tho' it seems incredible) of Southernmay, Dunston Rd. Old Headington writes to say that she has found the girl a room. The rest of your letter, she bears and all, I do remember—if it was the rest and not the whole. (For I was feeling as Johnson did about Burke "if I were to see Harwood now it would kill me".) As usual I can only thank you and wish I <u>could</u> come. Never fulfil the threat you once made of ceasing to ask me because I have so often refused. I live in the expectation of being some day a freer man and better friend: but not now. You know what driving an old car is like—the <u>normal</u> running becomes more and more abnormal and there is always a semi-crisis. My family life is like that: no-one's fault—just old age and the change in society wh. is depriving our own class of its "choregia." In other words, by the time my arm is out of a sling and I am able to face the journey (I couldn't at present) it will be high time for me to make myself useful at home: my prolonged status of "passenger" has already thrown heavy burdens on others. Thank Daphne a thousand times. Hospitality has in these days risen from the rank of courtesy to that of heroic virtue and I never knew anyone who had it in a higher*

Greek. One of the encyclic liturgies performed in ancient Athens, arranged and paid for by a kind of patron of a tribe or family.

degree. As to why my arm is in a sling—apparently when you remove a foreign body wh. has been so long naturalised, you sometimes get a "flare-up" of all the latent poison. I go to the Acland every day and have prongs stuck into it and the matter squeezed out of it. Don't pity me too much. The process looks revolting but, oddly enough, hurts no more than a lover's pinch. Nor is there apparently any danger to the arm. As for the stone which was removed from under my tongue, you will be pleased to hear that it must have impeded my speech all these years. So there's a good time coming. No more will you complain of that taciturnity wh. your kindness so often led you to attribute to modesty. No more will you whisper to Barfield after my rare remarks "If only he'd talk more."

(This reminds me of one of only two good things I found in M. Ward's Life of Chesterton, viz: on being told "Oh Master Gilbert you've got a little baby brother," G.K. replied "Now I shall always have an audience." The other good reply was to an American who asked him "Say, Mr. Chesterton, what makes women talk so much?" He answered, "God, Madam." But a dull book on the whole.)

I also read Martin Chuzzlewit and the second half of the Aeneid. M.C. is almost my favourite Dickens because in it the melodramatic parts (remember Jonas's drive to Salisbury with the man he means to murder) are almost as good as the comic ones. Aeneid VII–XII is pure gold: specially VIII. Can you read all this? My writing is *becoming no better than yours: partly because I have rheumatism in my right arm—that's the other arm. I'm writing to Mrs. Dodwell as soon as I've finished this. What do you think of Kipling? I have to talk about him in the near future. Am I right in thinking that the essential thing about him is neither patriotism nor imperialism but professionalism—i.e. he's the first man who has expressed the snug freemasonry between people who share the same work and the same hardship and grievances—the delight of talking shop when "we" are together and enjoy our unity against outsiders and also against the "cubs" and "pups," the "new bugs" in our own trade who aren't yet in the know. Up till Kipling fiction had been all about people's private lives: he first notices this immense vocational bond wh. is in some cases stronger than nationality, religion or family. The strength of his work comes from the fact that the thing he is talking about does really keep the "system of things" running every 24 hours and is responsible for countless heroisms. The sinister side of his work is that he doesn't seem to know (or perhaps care) that it is also the <u>modus operandi</u>—nay, the very incarnation, of nearly all strong corruption and cruelty. I shd. very much like (as Pecksniff says) to see your ideas on this. I read your sonnet and "Laura" to my literary friends recently. The sonnet, tho' not misliked, was completely overshadowed by "Laura" wh. everyone admired. Barfield is writing good things at present. I must stop now and write to Marcia D. My love, thanks and regrets to all.*

Yours truly,
C. S. Lewis.

My father was a very practical man and had a great love of carpentry.

This comes across well in his poem "Laura," to which Lewis refers in this letter and which reads as follows:

Laura

I took a plank of close-set grain,
      I made it smooth and good,
Foamed over from my gliding plane
      The crisp sweet curls of wood;
All day I worked them, pair by pair,
      Each plank its fellow sound,
A fence for my ribbed boat to wear
      And sail the seasons round.

With jointed posts I shaped the keel,
      I bored and pegged and strained,
Her helm was very light to feel,
      Her sail was russet-stained,
And on the taper mast I nailed
      A rood of ivory,—
But Laura begged my boat and sailed,
      And did not sail with me.

I gathered herbs from moor and field,
      Both root and leaf and bloom,
The rainbow colours they distilled
      I stretched upon my loom;
And there I made theme breathe again,
      I dewed their starry eyes,

And planted on that shining plain
    The tree of Paradise.

The tree that stood when Adam's breath
    Was life and love alone,
And Eva's had no taint of death,
    Upon my web had grown,—
But Laura came and looked and sighed
    And begged it for her shawl,
And left me, lovely in her pride,
    To scan an empty wall.

One other precious thing I had.
    Too dear to spurn or sell,
I groomed my little mare and bade
    Her carry Laura well,
Then turned my face from all I knew
    And vowed it good to part,
But ever as the long miles grew
    Her name was in my heart.

And O it sang so sweetly there,
    As though a rose should sing,
That words like bees made thick the air
    To sip that honeyed thing,
Till from my mouth it drew the breath,
    The song her name had made,
And riding homeward through the heath

She heard and stopped and stayed.

'O take me with you in your boat,
    Or set me on your mare,
Or on your woven web to float
    Poised in the dream-filled air.
Your song, like lightning from on high,
    Did shine my spirit through,
You gave me to myself—and I,
    Shall I give less to you?'

On another occasion Lewis and Barfield were enjoying the challenge of creating a philosophical alphabet. Lewis sent their first effort to my father, challenging him to complete the piece as follows:

A is the Absolute, none can express it
The Absolute! Gentlemen (fill up) God bless it.

M is the Many, the mortal, the body,
The formless, the female, the thoroughly shoddy

P is for Plato who thought that ideas
Were snobs who wd. only leave rinds on their peers

We've done as far as P, so let your higher thought
illuminate Q–Z.

The novelist and playwright Sir Compton Mackenzie was not a favorite author of Lewis's, a fact that seems clear from this damning piece which he sent to my father at about this time:

Lines to Mr. Compton Mackenzie.

Good heavens, Sir, will you condemn us
To talk of Romulus and Remus
And Venus—or perhaps Wenoos?
Each language has its native use,
And words like Saturn are abom-
inable here, if not in Rome.
Man, were you never taught at school
The genuinely English rule?
Antepenultimates with us
For the most part are shortened. Thus
<u>Crime</u>, <u>criminal</u>; and <u>rare</u> but <u>rarity</u>
(it rhymes in Thomas Hood with <u>charity</u>)
It's English, which you claim to love,
You're mangling in the interests of
A long-dead alien form of speech.
Learn your own tongue, before you teach,
And leave us meanwhile for our share
—The freedom of oure aine vulgaire.

6

GODFATHER JACK

It was in June 1933 that I was born. In spite of philosophical differences, my parents' friendship with Lewis was steadfast, and he was asked to be my godfather. The silver christening mug he gave me is dated October 21, 1933, and a letter to my mother sent on December 28 of that year alludes to this event:

Dear Mrs Harwood,

I don't know when I have been so rude to anyone as I have been to you after my long silence since I stayed with you. The truth is that if Cecil had not lent me Popelbaum's book I should have behaved better. I followed the ignis fatuus of postponing my letter until I could include some remarks on reading the book—then the time for reading the book didn't come as soon as I expected—and so here we are.

I have now read it and am very much impressed. A good deal of it, of course, is difficult to one so ignorant of science as I am, but it is all interesting and, I expect, deserves most serious consideration. Has any notice of it been taken in "orthodox" scientific circles? What particularly stuck in my mind—more as a tragedy than as a theorem—is the illustrated "rake's progress" of the Chimpanzee. What a subject for a poem! By the bye I have met a young philosophical tutor at New College (Crossman) who seems—which is rare at Oxford—to be well informed about Anthroposophy, and sympathetic tho' not converted. I think that is really more important for you than an out and out convert would be: it is a great point gained when a movement begins to be treated with respect by those who are not members of it. Incidentally, he is in several ways the most intelligent new acquaintance I have made for several years.

I hope you have not misinterpreted my long silence. I have the most grateful memories of my last weekend with you and value the novel honour of my <u>God-sibbe</u> very much. How is my godson? I hope his laughing all through the service does not mean that he is going to grow up an <u>esprit fort</u>: but as soon as he is old enough I shall try to collaborate with you in preventing this.

How is Stein?—a man I would like to meet again. And how is yourself and the <u>guideman</u> and the children? We are all pretty well, though Mrs. Moore is almost worn out with Christmas charities, which "an autumn 'twas that grew the more by reaping." We would all very much like to see you at the Kilns again when you can manage it. I have been disgustingly busy for a long long time: each year jobs seem to increase on one—as no doubt you find. Please give Cecil my love and accept all our best wishes for the new year.

Yours (penitent)
C. S. Lewis.

Jack became an assiduous godfather and remained in touch with me for the rest of his life. He wrote to me regularly, and his letters were superbly pitched to each stage of my boyhood development. At this time in his life his knowledge and understanding of children were gained through familiarity with those of his friends. I was only one of a number of godchildren; another was Owen Barfield's daughter Lucy, to whom he dedicated *The Lion, the Witch and the Wardrobe*. The dedication, charming in itself, reads as follows:

> *My dear Lucy,*
>
> *I wrote this story for you, but when I began it I had not realised that girls grow quicker than books. As a result you are already too old for fairy tales, and by the time it is printed and bound you will be older still. But some day you will be old enough to start reading fairy tales again. You can then take it down from some upper shelf, dust it, and tell me what you think of it. I shall probably be too deaf to hear, and too old to understand, a word you say, but I shall still be*
>
> *your affectionate Godfather*
> *C. S. Lewis.*

This dedication typifies Jack Lewis's warm and generous nature and simple modesty. My family all relished his visits to our home, where his jovial and erudite presence would immediately bring us joy and wonder. I well remember the frisson of excitement and awe of his presence, the laughter and bonhomie it created in the house, starting each morning with his booming voice shouting, "Bathroom free!" after he had completed his ablutions. When we were very young in Streatham, he always took his turn at pushing us vigorously and with gusto on our garden swing. He loved to swim and, when we lived in Sussex after the war, would often insist on an early-morning dip in the local lake before breakfast. He would be conversing incessantly with my father, sometimes even as he left the diving board for a belly-flop into the water. I was convinced that he could talk under water, because when his head eventually emerged, the words he uttered seemed to be several stages along the line of his thought. Much, probably most, of what he was discussing with my father went far above my head, but simply to be present and to witness their incomprehensible discourse was stimulating for a young boy.

Lewis would occasionally bring the discourse down to earth in a startling manner. For example, one day after he and my father had enjoyed a swim in the nude with my brother and me, he commented, "Very ugly things, aren't they, Cecil?" In answer to my father's "What things?" came his reply "Genitals, my dear man, genitals!"

As is evident from my earlier chapters, their discourse was kept alive in a regular exchange of letters. Lewis was a prodigious correspondent and once told me that he wrote on average seven handwritten (and wonderfully crafted) letters every day. I calculated that this must have amounted to more than 100,000 letters in his lifetime, not to mention the extraordinary fruitfulness of his pen as an author in so many other fields of writing. His practice was to destroy each letter he had received as soon as it was answered, so there is little evidence of what was written to him, for example, by my father save what can be deduced from the nature of Lewis's responses. Some exceptions to this general rule do exist, however, when (for example) he was commenting on some new piece of writing or a new poem.

Each Christmas Jack would send my father generous book tokens for books for me; a fine collection of Phaidon art books was accumulated over the years as a result. These I greatly treasured, in particular the tome on Botticelli. Once when ill in bed I asked my younger sister to fetch it up for me, with strange results. She reported to my parents that I required a bottle of jelly!

My godfather comments on the matter of choosing books for children in a letter to my mother written on January 6, 1939. She had recently returned from a visit to Jamaica with her father, Lord Sydney Olivier. He had been governor of Jamaica from 1907 to 1913 and had lived there in some style during that time with his wife and four daughters. Twenty-five years later they had paid a nostalgic visit to the island. It will be seen here that at this point Jack at last felt able to write on Christian-name terms to my mother; she must have offered him a bottle of rum from Jamaica and sought his advice about suitable books for me.

Dear Daphne,

Thanks very much for your nice long letter—I hope I have not thereby stolen time which ought to have been employed in the best of all occupations, and by you, perforce, the most neglected—doing nothing.

As a bachelor who has seldom even talked to children I should be very foolish if I gave any advice as to books for Laurence: if I felt qualified to choose books I should send books—not tokens.

But John is right about rum. It has a romantic interest. It is one of those things which give us a sensuous and an imaginative pleasure at once. And the only reason why I am going to refuse your very tempting offer of a bottle (or was it a keg? do say it was a keg—or a noggin) of rum is that it is your positive wifely duty to see that Cecil drinks it all. If he turns coy and altruistic and says (as men will say anything) that he doesn't care for rum, you may reply lightly in the Latin tongue <u>Hoc est omnis meus oculus</u>* or <u>Nonne narrabis ista marinis equestribus?</u>† He has not forgotten dancing through the streets of Caerleon with the bottle of white rum in one hand and his cutlass in the other. Of course for domestic purposes the question shd. not be put in a nakedly convivial way: some proper pretext about wet feet, overwork, or the like will do gentle violence to his coyness. But ye maun ablains give it to the guideman, ma'am.‡

I don't remember anything you said that day which could possibly offend anyone.

All here send their loves, and best wishes for the New Year. I hope it will be less exciting than the last but not with much confidence: one is reduced to the last form of hope now (I mean as regards this world) which consists in remembering that creaking gates hang long and things expected never happen. However, the prospect of leaving this planet gets daily less terrible. Tell Cecil to write to me some time.

Yours
Jack Lewis

PS I should say "having left." The modes of leaving do not much improve perhaps.

---

*"*This is all my eye!*" †"*Why don't you tell it to the Marines?*" ‡*An imitation of Scottish dialect: "Anyway you must give it to your husband, ma'am."*

Periodic correspondence between Jack and my mother continued, including the following rather special letter on the subject of "being in love," which he wrote to her in March 1942:

My view of being in love is that (like everything except God and the Devil) it is better than some things and worse than others. Then it comes on my scale of values higher than lust, selfishness or frigidity, but lower than charity, or constancy—in fact about on a level with friendship. Like everything (except God and the Devil) it therefore is sometimes opposed to things lower than itself and is—in that situation—good: sometimes to things higher than itself and in that situation—bad. Thus Being-in-Love is a better motive for marriage than, say, worldly advancement: but the intention to obey God's will by entering into an indissoluble partnership in all virtue and mutual charity for the preservation of chastity and the admission of new souls to the chance of eternal life is better than being in love.

So far it is fairly plain sailing. The trouble arises when poets and others set up this thing (good in certain conditions with its own proper degree of goodness) as an absolute. Which many do. An innocent and well intentioned emphasis on the importance of Being-in-Love with one's spouse (i.e. its superiority over lust or ambition as a basis for marriage) is in fact widely twisted into the doctrine that Being-in-Love sanctifies marriage and that therefore as soon as you are tired of your spouse you get a divorce. Thus the overpraising of a finite good, the pretence that it is absolute, defeats itself and corrupts the very good it set out to exalt; and what begins by wanting to go beyond the prayer-book idea of marriage ends by reducing marriage to mere concubinage . . . Treat "Love" as a God and you in fact make it a fiend.

*As to "Fate," which I call Providence, I believe that the coming together of a man and a woman, like everything else (e.g. the fall of a sparrow) is in the hand of God. In our society the matter is usually displayed in the form of mutual "falling in love." In the society to which our Lord spoke about "one flesh" this was not so; marriages were usually arranged by parents—and so in the vast majority of cases and places. I therefore cannot make "falling in love" the universal necessary pre-condition. We must always no doubt support it as against any inferior one, but not against any other one in general. As for Godson Laurence, if and when he asks me my views on the matter (a not very likely scene) of course I must tell him what I think true ***

As for "increasing Authoritarianism"—well! If that doesn't take the bun! When you have heard half as many sentences beginning "Christianity teaches" from me as I have heard ones beginning "Steiner says" from you and Cecil and Owen and Woff—why then we'll start talking about authoritarianism! I humbly trot out a few platitudes about marriage wh. cd. be paralleled in several moralists: you reply with an exact account of which species of angels are concerned in human love affairs! You may be right, and I wrong. But which is the authoritarian?

---

*At this time I was only nine years old.

Godfather Jack

93

As for austerity I see exactly what you feel and yet I don't think you've got me. I shd. hate you to believe that I am saying a word against love—or Poetry or Music or Friendship or even Wine. I think that of all of these we must say both "This also is Thou" and "Neither is this Thou." But people like you and me who have been cradled in poetry and suckled on humanism are in so little danger of forgetting the first and such daily danger of forgetting the second. It is so hard to express—I almost feel that Love is all poets claim <u>until</u> people begin saying so. "How like a god" is a man until he makes the fatal false step of claiming divinity and goes plumb down to devilhood.

And can one forget what sheer misery comes out of the divine (i.e. demonic) pretensions of romantic love—from Tristan *and* Anna Karenina *down to the last poor little suicide pact in the evening paper? And is it Being-in-love that really makes the happy marriage work? Isn't it something different—higher? Eros won't do without Agape.*

Yrs, Jack L.

My mother must have replied to this letter expressing some difference of opinion, as a further letter on the subject from Jack appears to indicate:

Dear Daphne—

I doubt if we differ as fundamentally as appears. I don't "pooh-pooh" any evolution in morals but neither do I know the future, and so I cannot say that the recent N.W. European development has come to stay, nor do I know whether it is an improvement.

I am also v. doubtful whether there is any intrinsic affinity between individuals as to make it certain that neither cd. have been perfectly married to anyone else. (It was neither savage nor cynic but that happiest husband and most inconsolable widower Johnson who replied—Cecil will turn it up for you—"Yes, Sir, With hundreds of thousands of other women".)

But my main feeling is, as I said in my last letter, that what we specially need to emphasise is the "Neither is this Thou" aspect. If one is taught to treat even religious emotion as a mere servant wh. must never be allowed to rule, how much more must one think this of erotic emotion!

All these things, on my view, are capable of <u>receiving</u> spiritual value but can't <u>give</u> it: and the moment they forget their <u>creaturely</u> status they become demons. I think the real difference between us is on a more general topic wh. I can't well go into now—I don't think the conception of <u>creatureliness</u> is part of your philosophy at all, and that your system is anthropocentric. That's the "great divide." (By the way I <u>have</u> had a letter from a civilised and married woman approving this point in Screwtape.*) Love to all.*

Yours truly, Jack Lewis

I recently discovered an old schoolboy diary of mine for the year 1949, written in a somewhat juvenile hand, at our home in Kidbrooke Park, Sussex.* On August 2 that year the diary records: "Father moved into John's room for Mr. C. S. Lewis my Godfather who was coming." And then: "Dr. C. S. Lewis came; jolly nice!" The diary goes on to record during the following days shopping in East Grinstead,

---

*My mother had been unwell so that my father was sleeping in his study; brother John was away.

swimming in the lake with Father and C. S. Lewis, and the fact that they went off to stay at the Dorset Arms in Withyham nearby before setting out on a walk together.

After this visit Lewis wrote the following bread-and-butter letter to my mother:

Dear Daphne,

It was all lovely and already seems very far away in the past. Thank you both very much for giving me such a good time—I don't think any other jaunt has done me so much good in every way. (Now that I've written it that sentence seems to make it sound as if it had been like medicine!—but that wasn't what I meant.)

I am venturing to send you an American parcel of which I get far more than my fair share. It's rather a dip in the lucky bran-tub for some contain really nice things like bacon and tongues and others contain such nonsense as paper-table-napkins or tinned pine-apples. I hope your dip will be lucky.

You've no idea what it's like coming back to a house in the middle of a building-estate after the sylvan glories of Kidbrooke.

Whoever finds my pencil may keep it! I got a new one in London with great difficulty. It is far below East Grinstead as a shopping centre; and the beer is not so good as at Withyham.

My duty to Lady Olivier; my compliments to Louis (?spelling?), my blessing and good wishes to Laurence; and my love to Sylvia, of which she may pass on any she does not need to the Rabbit family; and all these to Cecil and yourself with never so many thanks and wishes that

you will both have a really restful time at the Laytons (Leightons?
Latents?). NOTHING to the Duchess.

Your most obliged, Jack L.

On February 20 of the next year, 1950, Jack wrote what must have been one of his last letters to my mother before her death later in the year:

Dear Daphne,

You must have been bad if you thought last Wednesday was Ash
Wednesday—or else you hold some Columban and pre-augustinian
view on the date of Easter. (Your guideman will at a moment's
notice point out to you the passages in Bede which clear the whole
thing up.) I hope you're well now? Bronchitis is nasty enough.

Fry is shattering. I've seen none and only read The Lady's not for
Burning. *The funny parts were funny enough to make me laugh;*
as for the poetry—the wealth of real genius in the imagery is beyond
hope. Almost too much, and sometimes is rather splashed about than
used. But, by Gum, it's a good fault and one we'd almost despaired
of ever seeing again. Can it be—dare one hope—that the ghastly
mumbling and whining period in which you and I have lived nearly
all our lives, is really coming to an end? Shall we see gold and scarlet
and flutes and trumpets come back?

John is doing more this term. How is Sylvia? Give my love to
Laurence and all, including dear Woff. And take care of yourself: let
the young people work!

Yours sincerely, Jack L.

7

My Letters from
My Godfather

Once I had gotten old enough to write some simple letters to my eminent godfather myself, he took pains to reciprocate, and this was the start of a lifelong, albeit irregular, correspondence between us. His letters were always full of what he, rightly, judged would be of interest to me. In the early years they often contained charming marginal illustrations and sometimes puzzles to solve or secret writing to decode.

At Christmas 1944, toward the end of the war, I must have written to him with complaints about the cold weather, for he replied thus:

December 1944

Dear Laurence,

Thank you very much for writing me such a nice Xmas letter. It is very cold here too but I have not got so many colds as usual this year. I think it is because I have got a pair of very thick corduroy trousers,

My dear Laurence, thank you very much for
writing me such a nice Xmas letter. It is very
cold here too but I have not got so many
colds as usual this year. I think it
is because I have got a pair of very
thick corduroy trousers, so thick they
make me look like a Dutchman or
a sailor. I live in a college here: a college
is something rather like a castle and also
like a church. It stands just beside
a bridge over a river.
At the back of the part I live in
there is a nice grove of Trees. There are
a lot of Rabbits there. One very old rabbit is
so tame that it will run after me
and take things out of my hand.
I call her Baroness Bisket because
she is a kind of biscuit colour. There are also
stags and deer. The stags — I can't draw them
because their horns, which are called ANTLERS,
are too hard to draw — often fight at night

so thick they make me look like a Dutchman or sailor. I live in a cottage here: a cottage is something rather like a castle and also like a church. It stands just beside a bridge over a river. At the back of the part I live in there is a nice grove of trees. There are a lot of rabbits there. One very old rabbit is so tame that it will run after me and take things out of my hand. I call her Baroness Bisket because she is a kind of biscuit colour. There are also stags and deer. The stags, I can't draw them because their horns, which are called ANTLERS, are too hard to draw—often fight at night and if I lie awake I hear

and if I lie awake I hear the noise (click. click it goes) of their horns talking to gether. here I sit all day long writing books and letting examination kips... and letters. Somet we kill a deer to eat, the meat is called VENISON. Tell Daddy it is unrationed and I got a great big helping smoking hot the other night. I did enjoy myse but I wished he'd been there. I'm writing a story the Bear with a Bear in it at presen is going to get married in the last chapter, there are also Angels in it. But sometimes I don't thi it is going to be co

*the noise (<u>click</u>, <u>click</u> it goes) of their horns tapping together. So here
I sit all day long writing books and setting examination papers and
letters. Sometimes we kill a deer to eat, the meat is called* VENISON.
*Tell Daddy it is unrationed and I got a great big helping smoking hot
the other night. I did enjoy myself but wished he'd been there. I'm
writing a story with a Bear in it at present, the Bear is going to get
married in the last chapter, there are also Angels in it. But sometimes
I don't think it is going to be very good. I'm sorry you don't like
cold weather, I do, I love to see the frost all like sugar on the grass
and when it makes the fire burn bright. I'm sending you something
in this to get a Xmas box with. Well a very happy Xmas and lots
of love to Mark, Sylvia, Lois, John, Mummy, Daddy and yourself
from your loving godfather, Jack Lewis.*

Jack had become very fond of that particular biscuit rabbit, it appears;
in July of that same year, in a letter to his goddaughter Sarah Neylan,
he had confirmed this with the help of a charming limerick:

*I am getting to be quite friends with an old Rabbit who lives in the
Wood at Magdalen. I pick leaves off the trees for him because he
can't reach up to the branches and he eats them out of my hand. One
day he stood up on his hind legs and put his front paws against me,
he was so greedy. I wrote this about it:*

*A funny old man had a habit
Of giving a leaf to a rabbit.
At first it was shy
But then, by and by,
It got rude and would stand up to grab it.*

By the time he wrote to me at Christmas the rabbit appears to have changed its sex!

The subjects of weather and temperature often appeared in Jack's letters to me, most likely because these were often Christmas letters, when the weather was inclined to be inclement. Another example follows, written from the Kilns in Headington on January 3, 1946, when I was thirteen years old. The war was now over, and we had moved away from Minehead in Somerset and were newly established at Kidbrooke Park in Forest Row, Sussex.

> *My dear Laurence,*
>
> *Thank you very much for your nice letter and card. How I should like to see Kidbrooke, it sounds a lovely place, though in some ways I don't think it could be nicer than Minehead. As it is in Sussex, perhaps you will find the birds called yaffles.*

Jan 3rd 1946

Headington , Oxford.

My dear Lawrence

Thank you very much for your nice letter and card. How I should like to see Kidbrooke, it sounds a lovely place though in some ways I don't think it could be nicer than Minehead. As it is in Sussex, perhaps you will find the birds called Yaffles here. The pond is frozen over but not thick enough for skating yet. Our dog Bruce, who is very old and white-haired now, feels the cold very badly and has to be wrapped up in a blanket at night – he looks very funny in it. Yesterday

We are having very sharp frosts here. The pond is frozen over but
not thick enough for skating yet. Our dog Bruce, who is very old and
white-haired now, feels the cold very badly and has to be wrapped
up in a blanket at night—he looks very funny in it. Yesterday the
man who lives next door to us came into our garden when we weren't
looking and cut down one of our trees. He said it had elm-disease
and was spoiling his garden, but as he took the wood away with
him I call it stealing and we are very angry. He is an old man with
a white beard who eats nothing but raw vegetables. He used to be
a schoolmaster. He keeps goats who also have white beards and eat
nothing but raw vegetables. If I knew magic I should like to turn him
into a goat himself: it wouldn't be so very wicked because he is so
like a goat already! Don't you think it would serve him right? But I

cider. Do you wish you had been there!—or don't you like them
The stars have been wonderfully bright here lately. This house is so
funnily built that I have to go up to my bedroom by a rose
an outside stairway in the open air. As I go up Sirius (very
bright and green) looks as if he was sitting just on the top rail,
and then when I reach the top I see the whole of Orion. Orion. Can
out. Do you know any more? (I like Orion the best). I hope you
got a book token I sent you, but don't bother replying if you have
too many other letters to write. I have to write about seven a
day all the year round: isn't that dreadful? So I must stop
this one now and begin the next. All love and good wishes
to you and all the others for 1946,
          your affectionate godfather
                    C. S. Lewis

suppose he would then come over and eat the bark of the trees instead of cutting them down, so we should be no better off. The other thing I might do would be to challenge him to a duel but I suppose he is too old to fight and anyway I am not much good at fencing. Have you ever learned fencing? I think it would be nice. A few weeks ago I went into an inn near Oxford where the landlady gave home made ginger biscuits with my cider. Do you wish you had been there?—or don't you like them? The stars have been wonderfully bright here lately. This house is so funnily built that I have to go up to my bedroom by an outside stairway in the open air. As I go up Sirius (very bright and green) looks as if he was sitting just on the top rail, and then when I reach the top I see the whole of Orion. Orion, Cassiopeia and the Plough are the only constellations I can be sure of picking out. Do you know any more? (I like Orion the best). I hope you got a book token I sent you, but don't bother replying if you have too many other letters to write. I have to write about seven a day all the year round: isn't that dreadful? So I must stop this one now and begin the next. All love and good wishes to you and all the others for 1946,

your affectionate godfather, C. S. Lewis

Later that year a letter arrived dated August 26 describing with some amusement Jack's attempts to hire some French servants and taking up other subjects that he thought might be of interest to me:

My dear Laurence,

Thank you so much for your interesting letter and for congratulating me about being a Doctor. The most interesting thing about that was the place I went to to be made a Doctor—Saint Andrews. It is a

*most lovely little town with the sea breaking just under the windows
of some of the colleges. There is a ruined castle and a ruined cathedral
and miles and miles of sand.*

*One queer thing is that on this sand I saw no seagulls but lots of
crows! When I first saw them hopping about on the beach and
picking at the seaweed I said to myself "Hullo! Why are the gulls all
black in Scotland."*

*I would have answered your letter sooner but I have been very busy
these last few days answering letters from France. We are trying to get
two French servants, so we put an advertisement in a French paper
and these were the replies. They were all in French, of course, and
some of them were very funny. Many of the girls made quite as many
mistakes in French grammar as you or I would. (The French call a
servant a Bun and speak it Bonne.) I would like to see you in your
canoe: do you use a single or a double paddle? I have not had
much swimming this year because it has been so cold here.
But I still think swimming the nicest kind of exercise there
is (I think <u>standing</u>, just standing, the nastiest). This year
we have some of the queerest toadstools I have ever seen
in our wood, they are the colour of a tomato and have big
grey pimples on them. Perhaps you could tell me what
they are. I think your father must be having a lovely time
at Falmouth and I wish I knew how to get as many holidays
as he does! If I did I should soon come to Kidbrooke and ask
you to give me a sail in your canoe. Till then love to all.*

*Your affectionate godfather
C. S. Lewis*

On the last day of 1946 he wrote to me from Magdalen College, describing what he had observed in the countryside around Oxford:

My dear Laurence,

Thank you so much for your nice card and letter. I was glad to see a picture of the new Michael Hall,* having heard so much about it. It looks a beautiful place and I hope I shall be able to see it myself before too long.

Did you like the snow and frost? I did, except for getting up in the morning. We had our pond frozen but not strong enough for skating. I found this out in a funny way. There is a tree with a branch hanging down into the water which spoils one bit for bathing. I have always wanted to cut off the lower end of that branch but could never use a saw from the punt properly: so I thought "Now's my chance" and went out on the ice—and went through! Luckily I was near the bank so nothing worse happened than having to change my socks. But it is a horrid feeling when ice breaks under you!

It was rather nice here in the floods (did you have any?). The meadow outside my windows looked like a lake and the reflection of the trees in it was beautiful. Most of the deer had been moved into another field before the flood came but two had got left behind on a little island where there was just room for them to stand. They were very miserable until someone went and rescued them.

Talking of animals, a hedgehog came into our kitchen the other night. It didn't seem to be in the least afraid and drank a saucer of milk: when it had finished it got into the <u>saucer</u> and settled down to sleep just as if it intended to pass the night there! The chief other live

*The school.

stock in the garden is moles, toads and owls. I had a very fine view of an owl the other night.

Do you ever notice Venus these mornings at about quarter past seven? She has been terrifically bright lately, almost better than Jupiter.

Any news of John?* I enclose a book token with all good wishes for the new year and lots of love to yourself and all the others from

*Your affectionate godfather
C. S. Lewis*

Another Christmas letter dated December 23, 1947, arrived for me from Magdalen College and contained intriguing advice about a version of secret writing based on the Runic Alphabet:

Dear Laurence,

You'll wonder at the silly heading of this notepaper: but it is there because it is a present from an American who got it printed like that (I expect there are several Oxfords in America and he wanted it to be clear).

I wonder how you are all getting on? Nothing much has happened to me except that I saw a rabbit yawn. I suppose people who keep tame ones have seen it often but this was a wild rabbit and I thought it a v. curious sight. It was a very bored triangular yawn in the middle of a long hot afternoon.

I've also been re-reading Kipling's Just So Stories, *and have translated all the Runes round that picture of the tusk.*

**My brother at this time was in the Navy.*

In case you don't know the Runic Alphabet (which is a useful secret writing and supposed to have magical results) it is this:

ᚠ (A), ᛒ (B), ᚻ (c), ⊠ (d), ᛗ (e), ᚠ (f), ᛟ̃ (g), ᚷ ~ ᚻ (h), ᛁ (i), ᚦ (j), ᛣ (k), ᚱ (l), ᛗ (m), ᛏ (n), ᚠ (o), ᛒ (p), ᛦ (q), ᚱ (r), ᛍ (s), ↑ (t), ᚾ (u), ᚠ (v),

I am sure you will be able to read the secret parts of this letter, but whether you can read the ordinary bits is another matter.

Here's a Christmas box, that is, either ᚠ ᛁᛏᚱᛗ ᛪᛁᚠᛏ *or* ⊠·ᛦᛌᛏᛍ ᚪᛌ ᛦ ᛌᛏᚪ ᛌᛏᚱᛦᛌ ᚪᛌᛏᛦᛌ. *

Walter Hooper provides the following explanation of Kipling's book in note 128 on page 819 of *The Collected Letters of C. S. Lewis,* Volume 2:

There is a drawing on p. 141 of an ancient ivory tusk, with runes on both sides of the picture. Inside the copy of *Just So Stories* which Lewis was using, and which belonged to his brother, is a page of the proofs of *That Hideous Strength,* and written on the other side is the translation Lewis mentioned to Laurence. It is entitled "Transliteration of the Runes that face p. 140" and it is as follows: "This is the/stori of/Taffimai/ all ritten/out on/an old tusk/if u begin/ at the top/left hand/corner/and go on/to the right u can/see for/urself/ the

*"A iule gift or Nativity tr[i]bute."

things/as tha h/appened/the reas/on that I/spell/so k/ueerli is
b/ecause th/ere are/not eno/ugh let/ters in t/he runic/ alphab/
et for all the /ourds t/that I ou/ant to us/e to ou/belofed."

I was fourteen years old when I received this letter and became
fascinated with the challenge it set me. I have no recollection as to
whether I was able to unravel this cipher, however; if I did so, it was
doubtless with the help of my father. Neither history nor memory tells
me whether I was able to reply in kind to my godfather.

By a year later I must have become something of a bookworm
and told my godfather what I had been reading, no doubt in a rather
feeble attempt to impress him! His reply on December 29, 1948, tells
of his hatred of Dickens as a boy and his envy of my father for having
business that took him abroad. He poses a mathematical problem, and
he even seeks my advice on what he should read!

My dear Laurence,

*Thanks for your interesting letter. Instead of having a fat goose we had
a thin Turkey, so I expect you had the best of the bargain. We have
had a little ice on the pond but nothing near thick enough for skating.*

I shall be interested to hear what Lois thinks of Dartington Hall. I
once had as a pupil a girl who was a mistress there, and it seemed to
me that the more sensible that girl became the less she approved of
Dartington. (Perhaps you had better not hand that bit of information
on to Lois.)*

*What an excellent thing to have read nearly all the Waverley
novels.† At your age I had only read the medieval ones (Ivanhoe,
Q. Durward, The Talisman etc.) and didn't discover the more*

---

*modern ones (*Waverley, G. Mannering, Antiquary *etc.) till I was at Oxford. I now like those in the second list better than those in the first, but I think both lots very good and never get tired of them. What I like is that Scott doesn't skimp things, but tells you how everyone was dressed and what they ate and drank and what sort of houses they lived in, and the weather—which is what I always want to know though some people find it boring.*

I hated Dickens as a boy. I think the illustrations put me off. Long before I could read I used to turn them over and over as picture books, not liking them, indeed rather frightened by them, but fascinated. The very smell of that edition (you have noticed that every book has its peculiar smell: in fact the smell of some books, next to that of new shoes, is one of the best smells there is, I think)—the very smell of that edition had a sort of horror about it. Luckily I've got over it now and was re-reading Pickwick just before Christmas. But I've never gone back to O. Twist. Wd. you advise me too? Gt. Expectations is one of the best.

I have just read about a curious medieval method of proving your answer to a multiplication sum, and I am wondering if anyone at Michael Hall can explain why it works. I multiply, say, 12 by 63 and get the answer 756. I now want to find if I've done it right. I add the two digits of 12 (1 & 2) and get 3. I then add the two digits of 63 (6 & 3) and get 9. I multiply 3 × 9 and get 27. Then add 2 & 7 and get 9. Now I tackle the answer, 756. I add all its digits (7 + 5 + 6) and get 18. Add those digits 1 + 8 and get 9. The fact that I get 9 for both operations shows that my answer is right. Or here's another example:

13 × 22 = 286
13   1 + 3 = 4
22   2 + 2 = 4
Multiply 4 by 4 = 16
1 + 6 = 7
Add the digits in the answer: 2 +8 + 6 = 16
1 + 6 = 7

*Probably the explanation is quite simple and anyone less rotten at
Maths than I am will see it at once.*

*I rather envy your Father having "business" that takes him to
Switzerland. Mine never takes me anywhere half so nice: does
yours? You don't think this mysterious business, if we could follow
him (invisible) and watch, would turn out really to be tobogganing
and ski-ing and smoking cigars and having eight course dinners?*

*The cat keeps jumping on the chair and I must stop. I never knew
any animal so bad at taking a hint. Love to all and best wishes for
the New Year.*

Your affectionate Godfather,
C. S. Lewis.

The trouble Jack took to make his letters interesting to young people
has always struck me as remarkable given the very adult and academic
world in which he was living at Oxford and the pressure of his
working life as a don. Children were privileged to receive the benefit
of his observations and advice written in such a way that often set the
challenge of responding as best one could. Another godchild in 1949
was instructed thus about "what to do":

Remember there are only three kinds of things anyone need ever do. (1) Things we <u>ought</u> to do. (2) Things we've <u>got</u> to do. (3) Things we like doing. I say this because some people seem to spend so much of their time doing things for none of these reasons, things like reading books they don't like because other people read them. Things you ought to do are things like doing one's work at school, or being nice to other people. Things one has got to do are things like dressing and undressing, or household shopping. Things one likes doing—but of course I don't know what <u>you</u> like. Perhaps you'll write and tell me one day.

His knack of appealing to the very young shines through in this excerpt from a letter to a child written in 1950:

I just must tell you what I saw in a field—one young pig cross the field with a great big bundle of hay in its mouth and deliberately lay it down at the feet of an old pig. I could hardly believe my eyes. I'm sorry to say that the old pig didn't take the slightest notice. Perhaps <u>it</u> couldn't believe <u>its</u> eyes either.

And there was his wise guidance to a schoolgirl in America who had written (at her teacher's suggestion) to request advice on writing:

It is hard to give any general advice about writing. Here's my attempt.

(1) Turn off the Radio.

(2) Read all the good books you can, and avoid nearly all magazines.

*(3) Always write (and read) with the ear, not the eye. You shd. hear
every sentence you write as if it was being read aloud or spoken. If it
does not sound nice, try again.*

*(4) Write about what really interests you, whether it is real things
or imaginary things, and nothing else. (Notice this means that if you
are interested <u>only</u> in writing you will never be a writer, because you
will have nothing to write about . . .)*

*(5) Take great pains to be <u>clear</u>. Remember that though you start by
knowing what you mean, the reader doesn't, and a single ill chosen
word may lead him to a total misunderstanding. In a story it is
terribly easy just to forget that you have not told the reader something
that he wants to know—the whole picture is so clear in your own
mind that you forget that it isn't the same in his.*

*(6) When you give up a bit of work don't (unless it is hopelessly
bad) throw it away. Put it in a drawer. It may come in useful later.
Much of my best work, or what I think my best, is the re-writing of
things begun and abandoned years earlier.*

*(7) Don't use a typewriter. The noise will destroy
your sense of rhythm, which still needs years of training.*

*(8) Be sure you know the meaning (or meanings) of every
word you use.*

My oldest brother John went up to Magdalen College,
Oxford, from 1947 to 1950 while Lewis was a don there,
and Lewis became his tutor in English literature. A brief
letter to my mother written on October 20, 1947, from

Magdalen bears witness to this:

> *Dear Daphne,*
>
> *How nice to hear from you. About Being and Reason:—it is clear that something must be self-existent (wh. I take it is what you mean by "Being"). I claim to show that Reason must be self existent. There cannot be two independent self-existents. So I conclude that Reason is, or is a characteristic of, Being.*
>
> *John has returned beautiful as the day but not, I gather, having done much work in the vacation. Wonderful thing, this Heredity!*
>
> *When is Cecil coming to spend an evening and night again? Tuesdays and Wednesdays preferred. With good wishes to all.*
>
> *Yours*
> *Jack L.*

In December 1963, shortly after Lewis's death, Owen Barfield wrote to my father referring to this letter in connection with an obituary he was to write; he had not remembered it quite correctly, but his remarks are nonetheless apposite:

> *Have you still got Jack's letter about John ("It almost makes a chap believe in evolution")? If so, I might like, with your consent, to quote it in the Obituary I am going to do for the Oxford Mag. It is the best example I can recall of the peerless mixture of intimate allusion, personal affection, shrewd wit and pure fun, that sparkled in his letters to his friends.*
>
> *WSRUVWSR (="We shall rest, Uncle Vanya, we shall rest").*

*This was the kind of idiotic abbreviation Jack and I sometimes
indulged in. You remain the only conceivable recipient, so—
fashionable as the sport has no doubt become—I hope you will not
be in too much of a hurry to die.*

Jan 3rd 1946

Headington
Oxford.

My dear Lawrence

Thank you very much for your nice letter and card. How I should like to see Kidbrooke, it sounds a lovely place though in some ways I don't think it could be nicer than Minehead. As it is in Sussex, perhaps you will find the birds called Yaffles. We are having very sharp frosts here. The pond is frozen over but not thick enough for skating yet. Our dog Bruce, who is very old and white-haired now, feels the cold very badly and has to be wrapped up in a blanket at night – he looks very funny in it. Yesterday the man who lives next door to us came into our garden when we weren't looking and cut down one of our trees. He said it had elm-disease and was spoiling his garden, but as he took the wood away with him I call it stealing and we are very angry. He is an old man with a white beard who eats nothing but raw vegetables. He used to be a schoolmaster. He keeps goats who also have white beards and eat nothing but raw vegetables. If I knew magic I should like to turn him into a goat himself: it wouldn't be so very wicked because he is so like a goat already! Don't you think it would serve him right? But I suppose he would then come over and eat the bark of the trees instead of cutting them down, so we should be no better off. The other thing I might do would be to challenge him to a duel but I suppose he is too old to fight and anyway I am not much good at fencing. Have you ever learned fencing? I think it would b.. ... ago I went into an ...
gave me ...

The Kilns,
Headington Quarry
Oxford

4 Jan 63

Dear Lawrence   What a fool I am! Les pères de familles sont capables
de tout. There now does seem a chance— tho', drat it, not a certainty. But
the grinder we have in view will be able to take Douglas in the second
week or this month (it depends on the grinders sont G.C.E. results
which are not in till then). When I wrote to you I was trying to insure
against a whole wasted term. Which, you see, may still be necessary,
or which, anyway, will not amount to the 4 months you specify. So
there seems after all nothing you can do just at the moment. I may
have to pester you again some time. This preference is for doing
farming in my preference is for him to live en famille.

        Are you enjoying 1963 so far? We are not!

    A thousand thanks, and apologies,
                    yours
                        J Lewis

[envelope postmark: OXFORD 5 JAN 1963]

L. Harwood Ev.
    c/o 17, Pound Lane,

Ansd 24/165   Aylsham,

                Norfolk.

8

My Mother's Death

In May 1950 my mother was found to have cancer, and she was to die of this a year later. On hearing the news of the diagnosis, Jack Lewis wrote heartfelt and touching letters to my father; they are especially poignant in retrospect, as they almost seem to contain a premonition—his own wife, years later, would suffer the same end. Jack had lost his mother, his father and a favorite aunt to cancer, and recollection of those deaths no doubt imbued his words during this painful time in my family's life. In due course he would examine the pain of such loss very movingly in *A Grief Observed*.

> *My dear Harwood,*
>
> *I heard your terrible news from John this morning. I had hoped that you at least—you who alone of my friends always seemed to me, in any full sense of that word, happy—might be left so. You have been in that sense such a <u>rock</u> to us all, strong and solid. And I'm sure you will be still: but I hoped this mode would not be exacted. I have nothing to <u>say</u>: this letter is only a substitute for a look or a touch. I*

*suppose all that mere friends can do is to prevent (if they can do even
that) one very minor bye-product of sorrow, the sense of isolation
from the whole of one's old world, the feeling that all else goes on the
same. Believe me, it doesn't. Please give my dear love to Daphne.*

My older brother John got news of our mother's condition while at
Magdalen College as a pupil of Lewis's and wrote him a note to let him
know. Jack Lewis wrote him a most sympathetic response on May 9:

> *My dear Harwood,*
>
> *I can find no words to say what I thought and felt at getting your
> note this morning. When the same doom descended on my own
> mother I was a child, which made things worse in some ways, better
> in others; at any rate different: so I know I can't fully enter into your
> state of mind, still less your father's. You have had a rough passage,
> with a war to spoil the first part of your youth and then this. God
> help you.*
>
> *Does your mother know of her own state? I mean, wd. a letter
> to your Father raise any difficulties? It sometimes does at such a
> moment. Let me know.*
>
> *I always thought yr. Father the happiest man among all my friends.
> This somehow seems to make it worse—like seeing the highest house
> submerged by the flood.*
>
> *Yours C.S.L.*

Another letter to my father that soon followed, written on May 22,
included these words:

It is the apparent strength of my craft and the apparent lightness of yours that makes me so vividly aware of the stout captain in the one and the mere <u>Bellman</u> (see Hunting of the Snark)* *in the other. One of the bye-products of your news was to fill me with shame at the rattled condition in which I then was about troubles quite nugatory compared with yours.*

My hand (such as it is and so far as it can be) is always in yours and Daphne's. It is terrible to think (and yet how did one ever forget it) that unless in rare cases of simultaneous accident, <u>every</u> marriage ends in something like this.

God bless you all.

It was typical of my godfather's generous nature that he then wrote the following letter to my father, dated June 5, 1950.

My dear Cecil.

You know about that Trust of mine wh. Owen calls the Agapargyrometer? You must be incurring a good many unusual expenses at present: and there may be other—alleviations—you wd. like to incur for Daphne. Will you please write to Owen (he signs the cheques, not I) for any sums you want? The fund is in a most flourishing condition and there is no reason to stint yourself. You understand that nothing you draw impoverishes me, for all the money in that fund is already given away <u>from</u> me, tho' the question "To whom?" is answered at my direction from time to time.

We have so ruined the language that it wd. mean nothing if I said it "would be a pleasure." But reverse the positions and yr. imagination

---

This allusion is to the Bellman's speech in this Lewis Carroll book (author of Alice in Wonderland*).*

*will show you how very truly you wd. say, in my place, "it wd. be a
<u>relief.</u>" God bless you both; you are not often out of my mind.*

Yours Jack.

My father must have been persuaded to accept this selfless offer from
his friend as Jack's next letter confirms.

There then appeared to be some hope that the disease would not
be fatal, the news of which brought another sympathetic letter
from Jack to his friend:

*I can indeed imagine the heartrending pathos of this increasing
hope; and have often wondered whether our preference (in art) for
the tragic over the pathetic is not partly due to cowardice—that
the pathetic is unbearable. Still, one's frail agonies of pity and
tenderness don't fester and corrode in memory as their opposites
would. Still love to both: I wish it were of better quality—I
am a hard, cold, black man inside and in my life have not
wept enough.*

We were all of course devastated when my mother
died. The loss hit my brother John at a critical time, as he
was in the process of doing his final degree examinations,
including an oral exam (called a "viva") with Jack Lewis.
Lewis wrote to my father on August 8 expressing concern
for John:

My dear Cecil,

*Thank you for your letter which is one of the most <u>useful</u>
I have ever received. It brings home to me that aspect of*

*Death which is now most neglected—Death as a Rite or Initiation
Ceremony. And certainly something does come through into the
world, among the survivors, at the time and for a little while after.*

*I'm sorry about John's Class—and also that I feel I failed him badly
at our last meeting. I had been wondering for about 24 hours whether
the lightness of head and extreme lassitude that I was feeling were the
beginning of an illness. After a day in which I had had no leisure at
all and which had ended with a visit to the Nursing Home I had got
back to College feeling "all in." At that moment came his knock. It
was the moment of all others (between his mother's funeral and his
own viva) at which a chap might expect some moral support from
an older man even if that older man were not his tutor and a family
friend. But I could make no response at all. I'm sorry.*

*A weekend here, after your travels, can be arranged almost whenever
you like. Of course you will be thrice welcome.*

Yours ever,
Jack

My brother John, notwithstanding the above, was deeply appreciative of
Lewis as both lecturer and tutor; he says that in his lectures Lewis would
range widely over the subject matter and periodically summarize his
principal points. Some have described Lewis as bullying in his tutorials;
my brother attests that, on the contrary, "he would attempt to find some
merit, a glimpse of some ideas, in the pretty pedestrian essays that I read
to him. With great courtesy he would suggest that I should consider this
or that, extend my reading to include—whoever it might be. It was, in
fact, the general character of Lewis that, even if no more gladly than

anyone else, he would suffer fools with great patience."

When brother John left the University of Oxford he took up an international business career, but I feel sure that the influence of his tutor has stayed with him, given his love of literature and an ability with words that he has often demonstrated. For example, he sent this short, nostalgic poem to our father for Christmas 1963 from Colombo, Sri Lanka, where he was living at the time:

The snow lies thick in English hills
And in the lanes the drifts have blown;
Ice hangs, a sword, where water spills;
On window-panes frost-fronds have grown.

All through the night the snowflakes swirled
Muting the wind's shrill winter note,
They raced across the plains and whirled
Round mountain tops to lay their coat.

Now, in the dawn, the white land lies
Severe and shining in the sun
And on this Christmas day fear dies
And there is joy for everyone.

C. S. LEWIS
Magdalen College
OXFORD

8 / 8 / 50

My dear Cecil Thank you for your letter which is one of the most useful I have ever received. It brings home to me that aspect of Death which is now most neglected — Death as a Rite or Initiation Ceremony. And certainly something

MY FAILURE AT OXFORD

9

A year after my mother's death I entered my father's old college, Christ Church, Oxford, to study history. One of my tutors was the formidable Hugh Trevor-Roper. I was not a natural academic, however, and found it hard to make progress. After a year, I became seriously ill with double pneumonia, which held me back. The consequence was that I failed my essential preliminary examinations and left the University after only a year with little to show for it.

Although, in due course, this proved providential, I was devastated at the time and ashamed to have let down my father and my godfather. Rightly assuming that I would be miserable at this failure, Jack wrote me the most wonderful letter of comfort:

Magdalen; Aug. 2nd. [19]53.

My dear Laurence,

I was sorry to hear from Owen Barfield that you have taken a nasty

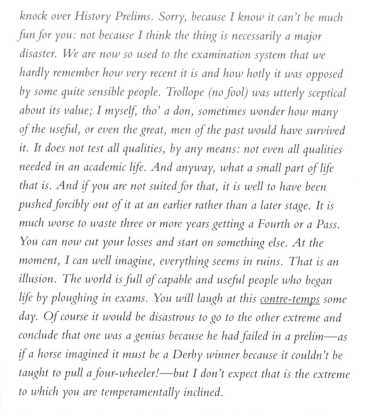

*knock over History Prelims. Sorry, because I know it can't be much
fun for you: not because I think the thing is necessarily a major
disaster. We are now so used to the examination system that we
hardly remember how very recent it is and how hotly it was opposed
by some quite sensible people. Trollope (no fool) was utterly sceptical
about its value; I myself, tho' a don, sometimes wonder how many
of the useful, or even the great, men of the past would have survived
it. It does not test all qualities, by any means: not even all qualities
needed in an academic life. And anyway, what a small part of life
that is. And if you are not suited for that, it is well to have been
pushed forcibly out of it at an earlier rather than a later stage. It is
much worse to waste three or more years getting a Fourth or a Pass.
You can now cut your losses and start on something else. At the
moment, I can well imagine, everything seems in ruins. That is an
illusion. The world is full of capable and useful people who began
life by ploughing in exams. You will laugh at this <u>contre-temps</u> some
day. Of course it would be disastrous to go to the other extreme and
conclude that one was a genius because he had failed in a prelim—as
if a horse imagined it must be a Derby winner because it couldn't be
taught to pull a four-wheeler!—but I don't expect that is the extreme
to which you are temperamentally inclined.*

*Are you in any danger of seeking consolation in <u>Resentment</u>? I
have no reason to suppose you are, but it is a favourite device of the
human mind (certainly of my mind) and one wants to be on one's
guard against it. And that is about the only way in which an early
failure like this can become a real permanent injury. A belief that
one has been misused, a tendency ever after to snap and snarl at the
"system"—that, I think, makes a man always a bore, usually an*

ass, sometimes a villain, so don't think either that you are no good or that you are a victim. Write the whole thing off and get on.

You may reply "it's easy talking." I shan't blame you if you do. I remember only too well what a hopeless oyster to be opened the world seemed at your age. I would have given a good deal to anyone who could have assured me that I ever could be able to persuade anyone to pay me a living wage for anything I could do. Life consisted of applying for jobs which other people got, writing books that no one would publish and giving lectures that no one attended. It all looks hopelessly hopeless, yet the vast majority of us manage to get on somehow and shake down somewhere in the end. You are now going through what most people (at least most of the people I know) find, in retrospect to have been the most unpleasant period of their lives. But it won't last; the road usually improves later. I think life is rather like a bumpy bed in a bad hotel. At first you can't imagine how you can lie on it, much less sleep on it. But presently one finds the right position and finally one is snoring away. By the time one is called it seems a v. good bed and one is loath to leave it.

This is a devilish stodgy letter. There's no need to bother answering it. I go to Ireland on 11th. Give my love to all and thank Sylvia for my bathing suit.

Yours.

This letter brought great consolation and reassurance to me, and I took the advice it contained and set off in a new direction. With funds that Lewis himself most generously made available, I was sent to the Royal Agricultural College, Cirencester, to undergo training as a chartered land agent and surveyor (surveying is the profession of land and estate management in the U.K.), which led in due course to a career with the National Trust. This was typical of Jack's enormous generosity. My father said that Jack's belief was that one should "give till it hurts," and he lived by this code all his life, often having insufficient funds for himself as a consequence. Owen Barfield recalled that he was wildly generous to all sorts of people: "He just scattered it. In the end, I put that right as his solicitor by a trust deed so that, thereafter, his gifts to individuals and charities came through me. Any of his friends were encouraged, if they knew of someone in need, to let him know."

In 1954 my father got married again, to Marguerite Lundgren, founder of the London School of Eurythmy. Until his death in 1975 they continued to live in the house he had designed and built in Forest Row, Sussex.

Magdalen
Aug 2ⁿᵈ 53

My dear Lawrence – I was sorry to hear from Owen Barfield that you have taken a nasty knock over History Prelim. Sorry, because I know it can't be much fun for you: not be- cause I think the thing is necessarily a major disaster. We are now so used to the examin- ation system that we hardly remember how very recent it .

10

Jack's Illness and Marriage to Joy Davidman

It was at the end of 1953 that Jack first mentioned to me, in a letter of December 21, the woman who was later to become his wife—Joy Davidman—and her two sons:

> *We have had an American lady staying in the house with her sons, eldest nine and a half. Whew! But you have had younger brothers, so you know what it is like. We didn't: we do now. Very pleasant, but, like surf bathing, leaves one rather breathless!*

Jack's civil marriage to Joy took place in April 1956 and was followed later, in March 1957, by a church marriage. The film *Shadowlands* portrays their courtship and marriage, their life together, and the period leading up to her death from cancer.

In 1957 Jack was recovering from an illness, and toward the end of that year Joy began to show signs of remission from the cancer that had plagued her. A letter to my father on September 21 confirms this:

My dear Cecil,

I am very much better. But I no longer take each period of pain for a permanent deterioration nor each free period for permanent recovery. They are both indirect results of the bone disease and of v. little symptomatic importance. I mustn't travel any more than I can help but shall be delighted to see you and Owen next term.

You needn't pity me too much. The <u>privative</u> side (farewell indefinitely, perhaps finally, to walks and bathes*) never worries me at all. Pain or even discomfort puts mere losses of pleasure quite out of account. What one can't do one soon ceases to want to do.

My wife has made wonderful progress, quite unexpected by the doctors. Can it be? . . . Dare one hope? I suppose not. But we are often a great deal happier, merrier, delighted, than you would think possible. We are at present being accorded all the privileges of shorn lambs.

Love to you both.

Yours,
Jack

Your letter warmed my heart.

In that same year, after completing my training at the Royal Agricultural College and qualifying as a chartered land agent, I had taken up my first job as a "factor" in the Scottish Highlands and must have written to my godfather to describe my life there. His regular Christmas letter, written on December 12, 1957, gives his response to this

---

*That is, going swimming.

and also makes reference to the remarkable recovery of his wife:

Dear Laurence,

*Thanks for your most interesting letter. I envy you your hills and
gillies and shepherds. I am surprised at your finding the Scotch (why
shd. I not call them Scotch even if they don't call themselves so? I call
the <u>Francais</u> "French," don't I?) less bookish, class for class, than
the English. I had always thought, and have sometimes found, them
more so. Pipes, in the open air, give me a strange pleasure, though
not perhaps a strictly musical one. More an affair of the nerves; they
are the only thing that makes me feel martial ardour.*

*All my news is good. My wife has made an almost miraculous,
certainly an unexpected, recovery. I myself am quite free from pain
again now. I have to wear a surgical belt, though: a thing like my
mother's or your grandmother's corsets! It's surprising how one gets
used to the contraption—except when one wants to <u>scratch</u> some
part which it covers.*

I enclose an offering. With love and good wishes,

Yours, Jack Lewis

In February 1959 Jack and Cecil planned a visit to Ely
together, and it appears that Joy was still well enough to
be included, to judge from this letter Jack wrote to my
father:

*Joy, now long disciplined in English cars wd. love a trip to
Ely on Wednesday or Thursday morning. But we don't
want you to come by car solely, if you prefer trains.*

I've just finished reading Cooke's Voyages. *Do you know who wrote these couplets?*

> *Slices the Natives brought of ham and tongue*
> *Where on each tree the ready breadfruit hung;*
> *Pleased with the scene, the Navigator smiles*
> *And names that happy clime the Sandwich Isles.*

The verse was, in fact, by Lewis himself!

Jack's wife, Joy, passed away on July 14, 1960; in April of that year they had managed to have a memorable holiday together in Greece, something which, for Joy, had been a lifelong ambition. Jack was distraught at her passing and wrote his powerful and harrowing book *A Grief Observed* to express his own experience of the great grief caused by his wife's untimely death.

1 1

JACK'S LAST YEARS

In 1960 I changed jobs and took up a post with the National Trust as a land agent in Norfolk, at about the time that Jack Lewis transferred from Magdalen, Oxford, to Magdalene, Cambridge, to serve as a visiting professor. In 1962 I wrote and asked if he would allow me to call him Jack now that I was grown up. We had been in correspondence about his stepson Douglas and what career he might follow. Jack was minded to consider land management training for him such as I had followed at the Royal Agricultural College in Cirencester; his reply to my letter alludes to this:

Dear Laurence,

(Yes, I'd much rather be called Jack. And also, like you, I've never discovered the plural of <u>syllabus</u>. Like <u>rhinoceros</u> and <u>genius</u>, it has "a thing about" its plural).

Your letter was not long-winded but heroic—for I know what dull work it is writing a long, clear account of what one already knows. Our present objective for Douglas is merely G.C.E.* as a preliminary for Cirencester.

A thousand thanks.

Yours, Jack

The Kilns,
Headington Quarry,
Oxfd

10 Sept 62

Dear Lawrence
(yes, I'd much rather be called Jack. And who, like you, I've never discovered the plural of *rhinoceros* and *genius*. it has "a thing about" its plural).

Your letter was not long-winded, but heroic—for I know what dull work it is writing a long, clear account of what one already knows. Our present objective for Douglas is merely G.C.E. as a preliminary for Cirencester.

A thousand thanks.
yours
Jack

**General Certificate of Education*

Because I was now living in Norfolk, so much closer to my godfather

Because I was now living in Norfolk, so much closer to my godfather in Cambridge, I was on several occasions able to visit him there to dine in hall with him and go on visits to the surrounding countryside. I remember one such occasion in particular when we went to Ely Cathedral, which he loved, and then partook of a bibulous lunch together. His two stepsons were growing up fast and causing him some concern regarding their future prospects. Our roles became reversed in a way as he sought my advice, particularly in relation to Douglas and his future career possibilities (one prospect was getting him some firsthand farming experience before attending an agricultural college). In this vein he wrote to me on January 4, 1963:

Dear Laurence,

What a pest I am! Ces peres de famille sont capable de tout. There now does seems some chance—tho', drat it, not a certainty—that the grinder† we have in view will be able to take Douglas in the second week of this month (it depends on the grinders' last G.C.E. results which are not in till then). When I wrote to you I was trying to insure against a whole wasted term. Which, you see, may still be necessary, and which, anyway, will not amount to the 4 months you specify. So there seems after all nothing you can do just at the moment. I may have to pester you again some time. His preference is for dairy farming and my preference is for him to live en famille.*

Are you enjoying 1963 so far? We are not!

A thousand thanks, and apologies.

Yours,
Jack.

---

*"These family fathers are capable of anything!" †That is, a tutor.

I think I may have been of some help, as the following letter of January 26, 1963, one of the coldest Januaries for a long time, explains:

> Dear Laurence,
>
> Yes, thank all good stars, we've got Douglas with a grinder at Godalming. I like the man's letters and he seems to think that D. now at last means business. But he has meant it so often before! Thanks very much for all your pains—you're more like a godfather (fairy type) than a godson. I may bother you about vocational work later on; we don't know any dates yet. We struggle on. Not all the pipes have stood up to it. Do you find it begins to make you very comatose—as if man were meant to be a hibernating animal? All the best for the New Year.
>
> Yours,
>
> . . .

This was the last letter I received from my godfather.

JACK'S DEATH

On November 22, 1963, the same day that President John F. Kennedy was assassinated in Dallas, Jack Lewis passed away. What a sense of loss I experienced on hearing of his death, as he had been a guiding light for me as my godfather throughout my life. I was now bereft of this light.

For my father, Jack's lifelong good friend and contemporary, the loss must have been even greater. Right up to his end they were exchanging poetry with each other and their friends. The following Lewis poem, one of my favorites, was dedicated to my parents and prefaced his book *Miracles:*

Among the hills a meteorite
Lies huge; and moss has overgrown,
And wind and rain with touches light
Made soft, the contours of the stone.

Thus easily can Earth digest
A cinder of sidereal fire,

And make her translunary guest
The native of an English shire.

Nor is it strange these wanderers
Find in her lap their fitting place,
For every particle that's hers
Came at the first from outer space.

All that is Earth has once been sky;
Down from the sun of old she came,
Or from some star that travelled by
Too close to his entangling flame.

Hence, if belated drops yet fall
From Heaven, on these her plastic power
Still works as once it worked on all
The glad rush of the golden shower.

I owe Jack a great debt not only for his considerable and caring influence on me as a godfather, as I have tried to show in this book, but also for his generosity in helping me toward a new vocational opportunity at a critical time in my life.

After Jack's death I remained in Norfolk working as a land agent for the National Trust for five more years. Thereafter I went up to Northumberland to direct the work of the Trust in that region for eleven years before transferring to Lancashire, Cumbria, and the Lake District until retirement. My thirty-six years with the Trust were extremely rewarding and gave me opportunities to meet a great variety of people and to be associated with some beautiful landscapes and buildings. To a large degree I owe this to my godfather, to whom this book is dedicated in gratitude for all he taught me and for all he gave me.

Since his death there have been many gatherings of Jack's friends and admirers to share memories of the man. At one of these at Magdalen College, Oxford, in July 1975, my father, who was himself to die in December of that year, gave a toast in memory of Jack, whom he, of course, knew so much better as a lifelong friend than I did as a mere godson. If it had not been for my father's friendship with Jack Lewis, I should never have had the privilege of being a godson to him. Thus as I began this book with descriptions of their friendship and activities together, I conclude it by quoting some passages from the tributes my father paid on that occasion to his great friend.

> Far more than Oliver Goldsmith did Lewis deserve the epitaph: *Nullum fere scribendi genus non tetigit: nullum tetigit quod non ornavit.** Literary and historical criticism, verse of many kinds, allegory, history, theology, Christian ethics and practice, planetary fiction, children's books—all came from his pen with equal readiness and in equal abundance. He had a teeming mind. When his fellow undergraduates were producing perhaps one exquisite lyric (now well forgotten) in a month, he was writing a young epic; and when he was told that one of its cantos was not up to standard he went away and produced another in the space of a few days.
>
> Like all who read his books—or were privileged to enjoy his conversation—I learnt very much from him, though others have made profounder studies in his works and been more deeply influenced by them. My own great debt to

---

*By Samuel Johnson: "Who left scarcely any style of writing untouched, and touched nothing that he did not adorn."

him—it could not have been greater—was that of an abiding friendship, which defied all differences of opinion, outlook and interests. I find that many of the experiences which live most vividly in my memory are those that I shared with him. I remember one of my early sojourns at the Kilns, when there had been a heavy fall of snow with no wind. We went out in the morning to a world transformed. Everything bore its replica in white. We tried to find words to express the beauty—the silence—of this new world, but ended speechless before it. At the other end of our meetings, on the last occasion when he was well enough to pay a visit to my home in Sussex, we were assailed after sunset by one of those tremendous storms when thunder and lightning were almost simultaneous and the whole house was wrapped in blinding flashes of light. We sat in a darkened room with open windows, overwhelmed by the sheer power of the elements. Jack said afterwards he had rarely been so frightened, and had never so much enjoyed being frightened. An almost equally memorable occasion was when I spent a weekend with him in Magdalen during the war. He had just discovered the works of that incomparable novelist of High Life, Mrs. Amanda Ross. We read one of her books to each other in turn until convulsions overcame the reader, and we ended by—literally—rolling together on the floor in one of those paroxysms of painful laughter which rarely visit one (alas) after one grows up.

He was at his best on walking tours when his delight in Nature vied with his enjoyment of conversation, in which of course he took a leading part. The day's walk had to be carefully planned so that we reached an inn about one o'clock—he held sandwiches in anathema as one of his printed letters testifies. There were grand tours with a muster of six or seven, but I remember well two or three walks we took alone. One was down the Wye Valley—then still a pretty remote place. As we came down from the hills to Tintern Abbey he shouted for joy that the hedges were still just as Wordsworth described them:

These hedgerows, hardly hedgerows, little lines
Of sportive wood run wild

Whenever I read those lines I hear Jack declaiming them as we strode down the hill. He lived in the present moment. No-one was less given to reminiscences—or to repining. I can hear him heartily deprecating all I have ventured to tell you about him this afternoon. He wrote me once that I should not be sorry for him because his illness deprived him of many things he had loved to do, because "you soon cease to want to do the things you know you can't do." And his interest was in people, not in institutions. That, I think, is why, when I read his works, I seem to hear him speaking to me. His benefactions, which were very great, were mostly to individuals, not to societies. He had enormous sympathy for the "little man." On one occasion when I was deprecating some modern housing estate, he said: "But if you could see not the houses, but the souls of the people in them, it might look very different." Indeed we shall never be true men "till we have faces." But I believe he felt that the simple man with his simple virtues might often be nearer that achievement than the sophisticated savant.

Jack had the rare ability to open windows for many people into realms hitherto unknown to them. No doubt he would have felt his greatest achievement was to open the windows of Christianity in a way no-one else had done in his generation. He has indeed opened windows for us all, or we would not be here. Let us drink a toast to his memory, in gratitude for what each one of us has received from him.

your affectionate godfather

C. S. Lewis

Image Credits and Permissions

Every effort has been made to secure permissions for copyrighted material. Any additions or corrections will be made in future printings.

Chapter 4: **Walking Tours**

p. 17 Lewis and friends, ca. 1933
Credit: Used by permission of The Marion E. Wade Center, Wheaton College, Wheaton, IL.

p. 18 "I am interested to inform you" (letter)
Credit: Courtesy of the C. S. Lewis Estate

p. 19 Illustration from letter
Credit: Courtesy of the C. S. Lewis Estate

p. 20 "The cottage called French Court" (letter)
Credit: Courtesy of the C. S. Lewis Estate

p. 23 Lewis and friends, ca. 1933
Credit: Used by permission of The Marion E. Wade Center, Wheaton College, Wheaton, IL.

p. 25 Well-fed young Lewis at Stonehenge, ca. 1935
Credit: Used by permission of The Marion E. Wade Center, Wheaton College, Wheaton, IL.

p. 26 Owen Barfield
Credit: Courtesy of the author

p. 28 Capt. W. O. Field (Wof)
Credit: Courtesy of the author

p. 31 Lewis with walking stick, ca. 1938
Credit: Used by permission of The Marion E. Wade Center, Wheaton College, Wheaton, IL.

p. 32 Owen Barfield and Cecil Harwood (detail)
Credit: Courtesy of the author

p. 33 "O Caecili care jam" (note)
Credit: Courtesy of the C. S. Lewis Estate

p. 34 Owen Barfield (detail)
Credit: Courtesy of the author

p. 35 Cecil Harwood (detail)
Credit: Courtesy of the author

p. 36 Lewis the student, after returning from war, ca. 1919
Credit: Used by permission of The Marion E. Wade Center, Wheaton College, Wheaton, IL.

p. 38 Laurence Harwood and siblings, Mark and Sylvia
Credit: Courtesy of the author

Chapter 5: Friendship After Oxford

Image Credits and Permissions

p. 140 Lewis reading, ca. 1958
Credit: Burt Glinn/Magnum Photos

p. 141 "Your affectionate godfather" (salutation)
Credit: Courtesy of the C. S. Lewis Estate